TOTALLY COMMITTED
TO CHRIST

TOTALLY COMMITTED TO CHRIST

Being a faithful steward of God

Brian A. Russell

EVANGELICAL PRESS

 EVANGELICAL PRESS

Evangelical Press
Faverdale North, Darlington, DL3 0PH England
Evangelical Press USA
PO Box 825, Webster NY 14580 USA
email: sales@evangelical-press.org
www.evangelicalpress.org

'The Guide' web site: **www.evangelicalpress.org/TheGuide**

Published by Evangelical Press
First published 2004

British Library Cataloguing in Publication Data available
ISBN 0 85234 570 4

*Affectionately dedicated
to my three children,*

Renelle, Haydn and Melanie

*The unsearchable riches of Christ
are the only lasting inheritance
I can leave you.*

ACKNOWLEDGEMENTS

I would like to express my thanks to:

- Erroll Hulse, whose physical and spiritual roots (like mine) were in South Africa, for persistently encouraging me to write on Christian stewardship. It was his vision that gave birth to this book.
- The editorial board of Evangelical Press for the many valuable suggestions that they have made to improve the manuscript.
- My wife Muriel, who has typed and retyped this manuscript and so devotedly done all my typing for the past forty-five years. My life would be the poorer without her.

CONTENTS

FOREWORD

When Zaccheus, a wealthy man, was called by Jesus, he expressed his love immediately by dedicating half his possessions to the poor. This is very unusual. It reminds us that conversion represents a profound change. It is a calling from darkness to light and from the power of Satan to God. It is the gift of eternal life. The new convert is full of zeal to show gratitude. That is the best time to learn how to become a faithful steward. I wonder what I would have thought of this book if I had read it in the days following my own conversion? However, this book is not just for new believers. It will challenge all Christians, the most experienced as well as those who are young in the faith.

Brian Russell and I come from the same background in South Africa. When my wife and I were converted we were taught discipleship without delay. Inculcated from the beginning was the principle of never missing the weekly church prayer meeting, a practice we have maintained for fifty years. This assertion is not to make us appear better than others. On the contrary, the personal benefits that accrue from that practice are beyond human calculation. The same applies to the principle of devoting the whole of the Lord's Day to spiritual worship and service. We were taught that as well and also the importance of tithing, the need to witness to our faith and the need to serve.

These are only some aspects of stewardship. Pastor Russell goes to the heart of the matter by establishing the principle of grace. From there he expounds the stewardship of the body and of the mind. In a postmodern generation in which television predominates, the importance of the spiritual discipline of the mind can hardly be exaggerated. This is followed by an exciting chapter in which we are brought to admire the variety of gifts given by God to individuals, all of which are to be put to use in the kingdom of God. That very precious commodity of time is examined with much profit and practical application.

I will not comment on all the chapters except to make the observation that while we greatly value books on systematic theology, none of them deal with daily practical living like this book does. Every chapter concludes with questions and with prayer.

A feature of this work is the use of hymns. This is not surprising as Brian Russell's love for hymnology has played a significant part in his ministry. I noted when I came to chapter three that the hymn 'Take my life and let it be, consecrated

Lord to Thee' by Frances Ridley Havergal is quoted in full. We chose this hymn for our wedding service. We enjoy hymns both old and new and favour the use of contemporary language. However, hymns like the one just referred to defy modernization and will not bend to transposition into modern style.

I am delighted to know that this book will be available and heartily commend it to all, but especially to pastors who will want to use many copies for the benefit of church members, and to challenge those who profess to be Christians but who for one reason or another keep themselves on the circumference of church life.

Erroll Hulse
Leeds, UK
September 2004

Your salvation is God's business; his service your business.
— *Thomas Fuller*

Unless a man's faith saves him out of selfishness into service, it will never save him out of hell into heaven.
— *Mark Guy Pearce*

Christian service has been dignified by Deity.
— *John Blanchard*

You do not do God a favour by serving him. He honours you by allowing you to serve him.
— *Victor Nyquist*

Since my heart was touched at seventeen, I believe I have never awakened from sleep, in sickness or in health, by day or by night, without my first waking thought being how best I might serve my Lord.
— *Elizabeth Fry*

If the service of God is worth anything, it is worth everything.
— *C. H. Spurgeon*

No reservations. No regrets. No retreat.
— *David Livingstone*

You will certainly carry out God's purpose, however you act; but it makes a difference to you whether you serve like Judas or John.
— *C. S. Lewis*

INTRODUCTION

We often say in ordinary conversation that there is no room as big as the room for improvement. They are wise words and are especially true of our consecration and service to God, our Creator and Redeemer, who has absolute rights over all we are and have; for we are his twice over. First, he made us in his likeness with every ability to serve him as perfectly as do the angels in heaven, except that having physical bodies, we do require rest at night. Second, when we sold ourselves as 'instruments of unrighteousness to sin' and became the 'slaves of sin' (Rom. 6:13,17), God in the person of his Son, Jesus Christ, came to earth and gave his life to ransom us from that terrible evil bondage (Mark 10:45). And 'now having been set free from sin, and having become slaves of God' (Rom. 6:22), we should be totally committed to serving him to whom we literally owe all.

But sadly, no honest observer of Christian churches in the affluent and materialistic West today will disagree with me when I say that a significant majority of the members of these churches are largely uncommitted to

God and his service. Nor will the remaining members, who are trying with God's help to serve him acceptably, make any pretense of being satisfied with their own performance. For they sincerely endorse the words of their Lord and Saviour in Luke 17:10: 'So likewise you, when you have done all those things which you are commanded, say, "We are unprofitable servants. We have done what was our duty to do."' All Christians everywhere, by reason of continuing indwelling sin, have a daily struggle to serve God as he deserves.

Whether we are those who are striving to do better or those who are slacking off because of our preoccupation with the things of this life, we need to turn afresh to God's written Word for instruction and exhortation on how and why we should be more faithful stewards of God. With a dire shortage of dedicated workers, the contemporary Western church is lurching forward like an eight cylinder engine firing on only two cylinders. In proportion to the number of its official members its efforts to do the will of God are shamefully feeble.

I can only speak from my own experience, which is very limited indeed, but in my forty-one years of pastoral ministry in six churches in South Africa, Zimbabwe and the USA, my observations have been largely the same. The bulk of the Lord's work is being done by a small core of spiritually dedicated members numbering not more than a quarter to one-third of the resident membership. This finding is confirmed by ministerial friends serving in America, Canada, Britain, Europe, Africa and Australia. It is also borne out by denominational statistics in all of these countries.

Take the Southern Baptist Convention in which I currently serve. Their 2001 annual report reflected that they had 16,052,920 members baptized on a profession of faith and total receipts of US $8.3 billion — which means that each member gave to their church an average of US $518 per year. If they were tithing, their average annual income would only have been US $5,180, which is US $15,000 below the poverty level. The per capita giving of Southern Baptists to international missions was US $12.89 and US $5.60 to home missions (this takes into account budgeted giving as well as Christmas and Easter special offerings). That same year Southern Baptists had 5,154 home missionaries and 5,100 international missionaries — which works out to one missionary for every 1,566 members. More alarming is the fact that the average Sunday morning worship attendance was 5,730,980 — just over one-third of the total average membership. When assessing these statistics, it is important to remember that the Southern Baptist Convention is the largest Protestant denomination in America, supporting the largest Protestant denominational missionary society in the world. The situation in other denominations in the West will surely be even more dismal. In Britain and Europe they are absolutely abysmal.

The following satire is not too far off the mark. It appeared in a local church newsletter.

Our church has a membership of 87 persons. Of these, 27 are away in the army or at college, leaving only 60 to do the Lord's work. Of these 60 people, 25 are elderly, ill or otherwise incapacitated in some way, leaving only 35 people to do the Lord's work. A further 15 people have indicated that they have done their share, leaving 20 to carry the work of the Lord on their shoulders. Of these 20, 15 are totally absorbed in their jobs, homes or hobbies, leaving only 5 to shoulder the responsibility. 3 of these feel that they have no gifts or talents to use. That leaves 2 people to do all the work, and that is you and me, brother, and I am getting sick and tired of doing everything myself. So get off your chair and pull your weight.
Author unknown — and probably prematurely deceased

It seems to me, then, that while all Christians rejoice in their status as the 'children of God', not many are as eager to take seriously the fact that they are also by grace the 'stewards of God'. Such a choice is not permissible. With privilege comes responsibility. That is true of both earthly sonship and divine sonship. No Christian may be excused from his or her responsibility to use the resources given them for the glory of God and the good of their fellow believers. To waste God's resources on myself is the height of folly. As Martin Luther wisely observed: 'I have had many things in my hands, and have lost them all; but whatever I have been able to place in God's hands I still possess.'

Although there is little that is new in this book on Christian commitment, it is an attempt under God's prompting and enabling to address the serious problem of unfaithful stewardship that is evident in so many churches today. It is my prayer that this simple, straightforward presentation of the biblical doctrine of stewardship will be used by the Holy Spirit, our heavenly Teacher, to challenge you, the reader, to be a faithful steward of the bountiful resources that God, in his grace, has entrusted to you. God's Word is spiritually transforming when we allow it to sink deep into the heart of our being. As Jesus said, 'If you abide in my word, you are my disciples indeed. And you shall know the truth, and the truth shall make you free' (John 8:31–32).

Brian A. Russell
Cobbs Creek, Virginia, USA
September 2004

HOW TO USE *THE GUIDE*

Totally committed to Christ is latest in a series of books called *The Guide*. This series covers books of the Bible on an individual basis, such as Ecclesiastes and Job, and relevant topics, such as creation and Christian comfort. The objective of the series is to communicate the Christian faith in a straightforward and readable way and encourage believers to live our their faith.

To help you to study the Word of God more deeply, each book in *The Guide* series has relatively short and concise chapters with questions at the end of each chapter for personal study or group discussion.

An innovative and exciting feature of *The Guide* is that it is linked to its own web site. As well as being encouraged to search God's Word for yourself, you are invited to ask questions related to the book on the web site, where you will not only have your own questions answered, but you can also see a selection of answers that have been given to other readers. The web site can be found at *www.evangelicalpress.org/TheGuide*. Once you are on the site you just need to click on the 'select' button at the top of the page and choose the book on which you wish to post a question. Your question will then be answered either by Michael Bentley, the web site coordinator and author of *Colossians and Philemon*, or others who have been selected because of their experience and understanding of the Word of God and their dedication to working for the glory of the Lord.

There are other titles in line to be published in *The Guide* series and with the positive feedback and popularity of our interactive web site, we hope to continue that into the future.

It is the publisher's hope that you will be stirred to think more deeply about the Christian faith and that you will be helped and encouraged — through the study of God's Word — in living out your Christian life. We live in demanding days and we need the firm compass of the Word of God to give us direction and practical encouragement as we navigate the complexities of this new millennium and pursue the glory of our God.

www.evangelicalpress.org/TheGuide

All for Jesus! All for Jesus!
    All my being's ransomed powers;
All my thoughts and words and doings;
    All my days and all my hours.

Let my hands perform His bidding;
    Let my feet run in His ways;
Let my eyes see Jesus only;
    Let my lips speak forth His praise.

Worldlings prize their gems of beauty;
    Cling to guilded toys of dust;
Boast of wealth and fame and pleasure;
    Only Jesus will I trust.

Since my eyes were fixed on Jesus,
    I've lost sight of all beside;
So enchained my spirit's vision,
    Looking at the Crucified.

Oh, what wonder! how amazing!
    Jesus, glorious King of kings,
Deigns to call me His beloved,
    Lets me rest beneath His wings.

— *Mary D. James (1810–1883)*

THE GUIDE

CHAPTER ONE

WHAT IS A STEWARD OF GOD?

LOOK IT UP

BIBLE REFERENCE

Let a man so consider us, as servants of Christ
and stewards of the mysteries of God. Moreover it is
required in stewards that one be found faithful
(1 Cor. 4:1–2).

I beseech you therefore brethren, by the mercies of
God, that you present your bodies a living sacrifice,
holy, acceptable to God, which is your reasonable
service... not lagging in diligence, fervent in spirit,
serving the Lord (Rom. 12:1,11).

INTRODUCTION

After the horrific destruction of the World Trade
Center in New York on 11 September 2001 by
Muslim terrorists, a person being interviewed on
American television said, 'The most dedicated
people in the world are Muslim fundamentalists.'
It would be difficult to refute that claim, ill-
guided as such dedication may be. The world
would be a different place if all Christians were
equally and biblically dedicated to serve the
supreme cause of Jesus Christ at all costs. Where
is the total commitment and daring sacrifice of the
early Christians following the day of Pentecost?

Where indeed? J. B. Phillips in the preface to
his paraphrase of the book of Acts speaks of that
first century as the time before the church
'became fat and short of breath through pros-
perity, or muscle-bound by over-organization'.

Partial consecration is the blight of Christian disciple-ship today. God is asking for *all*, and every one of us is tempted to buy him off with something less (Rom. 12:1,11; 1 Cor. 15:58; Rev. 3:14–22).

Early one morning in Dublin in 1867 a group of men gathered for a season of special prayer, confession and renewed dedication. Among them were Grattan Guinness, Henry Varley and D. L. Moody. During a hushed interval Varley said, 'The world has yet to see what God can do with and through and in a man who is fully and wholly consecrated to Him.'

Moody was greatly moved by this remark and two days later, as he sat listening to one of God's great servants, C. H. Spurgeon, Varley's words were still going through his mind. This is Moody's own account of what happened:

A man! Varley meant *any* man. Varley didn't say he had to be educated or brilliant, or anything else! Just a man! 'Well', said Moody, 'by the Holy Spirit, I want to be one of those men.' And as he sat in that high gallery, he saw something he had never realized before. It was not Spurgeon who was doing the work of moving men's hearts; it was God. 'And if God could use Mr. Spurgeon', he thought, 'why should He not use the rest of us? And why should we not all just lay ourselves at the Master's feet, and say to Him: "Send me, Lord! Use me!"'

God may not use us in the same way that he used Spurgeon or Moody, but if we fully dedicate our lives to

EXPLANATION

his service, he will use us in a way beyond anything we are doing now, the results of which only eternity will reveal. Why are we so loathe to give ourselves completely to the glorious service of our loving and just heavenly Master, especially knowing that what we achieve will be eternal 'treasures in heaven where neither moth nor rust destroys and where thieves do not break in and steal' (Matt. 6:19)?

Make no mistake, it is a responsibility from which we cannot escape. We cannot deny it. No Christian has the luxury of being able to say, 'I am happy to be a child of God. I am delighted to be an heir of God, but I would rather not be a steward or servant of God.' We do not have that option. We cannot be excused from our responsibility to use the gifts God has given us for his glory.

Well then, what is a steward of God? The use of the word 'steward' to describe a Christian is used three times in the Gospels (Matt. 24:45; Luke 12:42; 16:1) and four times in the epistles of Paul and Peter (1 Cor. 4:1–2; Titus1:7; 1 Peter 4:10).

The etymology of the word 'steward'

The word steward in our English New Testament is the translation of the Greek word *oikonomos*, which is made up of two separate words. The first, *oikos*, means a house and the second, *nemo*, means to dispense or manage. The *oikonomos*, there-fore, was the housekeeper of a rich man's house and his office is termed *oikonomia*, which is translated as stewardship in Luke 16:1–9. The householder or 'master of the house' is called *oikodespotes* and the other servants of the household are termed *oiketai*.

A steward in the Bible, then, is the manager who has been put in charge of his master's house, the people living in the house and his goods. Today we usually think of a steward as someone in charge of union members at a factory or serving food and drinks on a train or plane, but the sense is still the same. A steward is someone who is in charge of property belonging to somebody else and his duty is to dispense the master's goods for the benefit of other people who are important to his master.

Oikonomos is defined in Grimm and Thayer's lexicon as: 'The manager of a household or of household affairs; especially a steward, manager, superintendent... to whom the head of a house or proprietor has entrusted the management of his affairs, the care of receipts and expenditures, and the duty of dealing out the proper portion to every servant and even to the children not yet of age.' So whether the *oikonomos* was a free man or a slave, he occupied a responsible position between the householder and his household. The stewards in Matthew 24:45 and Luke 12:42–43 are called slaves, whereas the unjust steward in Luke 16:1–9 seems to have been a free man. Indeed, in Romans 16:23 the word is used in that sense of Erastus who was the 'treasurer' of the city of Corinth and obviously a free man. Moreover, in Galatians 4:2 a child in a well-to-do home is said to be under both an *epitropous* (called a steward in Matthew 20:8) and an *oikonomous*, the former being his legal guardian, whereas the latter would have been in charge of his property.

But before we end the etymological lesson, we need to look at the suitability of our English translation of the Greek word *oikonomos*. Is the word steward a good translation? Yes, it is. The word steward comes from the old English word *stiward*, which is also made up of two words. The word *sti* is a shortened form of the old word *stig* which referred to some form of a house. The nearest word we have from this root today is the word *sty* as in *pigsty*. The other word making up our English translation is *ward* (someone who takes care of something or someone). So in putting those two words together (steward) we have a very good translation of the original.

Biblical examples of stewardship

The concept of the household steward was more familiar in Bible times than it is in ours. We associate the word stewardship with campaigns to raise money for the church. But in the ancient Middle East every prosperous householder or farmer had a steward to manage his household affairs and his property as we have seen from our study of the Greek words concerned. In the Old Testament there are many examples of functioning stewards. No single Hebrew word is used to identify him, but his office is referred to in several words, and he can be seen in the noble families and royal courts of Egypt, Judah and Babylon.

For example, Joseph had a steward when he was, as it were, the prime minister of Egypt. This 'steward of his house' (Gen. 43:16–25) was charged with looking after Joseph's brothers. He was responsible for slaughtering an animal and preparing a meal for them. He also gave them water to wash their feet, fodder for their donkeys and received the money that they brought to pay for the grain (Gen. 44:1–13).

Similarly, David had officials who are described in 1 Chronicles 28:1 as 'the stewards over all the substance and possessions of the king and his sons'. According to Isaiah 22:15 King Hezekiah had a steward named Shebna who enriched himself at the expense of the royal household account. But God tells Shebna that he is to be replaced by Eliakim. 'I will commit your responsibility into his hand. He shall be a father to the inhabitants of Jerusalem and to the house of Judah. The key of the house of David I will lay on his shoulder; so he shall open, and no one shall shut; and he shall shut, and no one shall open' (Isa. 22:21–22). In other words, he shall have the key to the king's storehouse.

Again, in King Nebuchadnezzar's court at Babylon, the chief of the eunuchs put Daniel and his three companions in the care of a steward (Dan. 1:11). We are also told that it was his task to train young men to serve in the palace and to issue them with daily rations that, at his discretion, could be the rich food and wine of the court or the plain vegetables and water for which Daniel asked.

When we come to the New Testament the role of the steward does not change. Herod Antipas had a steward at court called Chuza, whose wife, Joanna, was a disciple of Jesus and helped to provide for her Saviour from her substance (Luke 8:3). But more to the point, the scene in several of our Lord's parables is set in a great household in which the steward occupies a position of responsibility. In the parable of the labourers in the vineyard (Matt. 20:1,8) the steward is ordered by the owner of the vineyard to pay the labourers their wages. In the parable of the unjust steward (Luke 16:1–9) the steward is accused by his master of wasting his goods. He is clearly a man in a position to order provisions for the household and pay the bills because he is able to falsify the accounts for his own benefit.

The New Testament use of this term

With this background we are now in a position to understand what our Lord Jesus and his apostles meant when they spoke of Christians as 'stewards of God' (Luke 12:42; 1 Cor. 4:1; 1 Peter 4:10). They were led by the Holy Spirit to see in this social pattern a picture of the Christian church. With

God as 'our Father' (Matt. 6:9) it was natural to think of
the Christian family as being 'members of the household of God' (Eph. 2:19). But the picture is not rigorously
pressed, for although God is always the householder, the
church is sometimes the house or temple in which he
dwells (1 Tim. 3:15; 1 Peter 4:17; 1 Cor. 3:16) while at
other times it is his 'household of faith' in which his
sons and daughters are servants and are responsible to
him for their work (Rom. 14:4).

So the New Testament usage of the term 'a steward
of God' is not uniformly consistent. There are times
when it follows the strict meaning of the term in
which every house had only one steward who was
charged with supervising and taking care of all the
other servants in his master's household. Paul uses the
term in this sense when he speaks of an elder or pastor
as 'a steward of God' in Titus 1:7. In 1 Corinthians 4:1
he says that he and Apollos (and by implication any
other preacher) should be regarded as 'stewards of the
mysteries of God'.

The steward here is clearly a descriptive title for all
who have the privilege of preaching God's Word to the
church. And 'the mysteries of God' which Christian
ministers are to preach, are the truths of salvation by
grace alone, through faith alone, in Christ alone that
were previously hidden from men. But God in his goodness, not wishing that anyone should perish, has made
these truths known by revealing them through the Holy
Spirit to his prophets and apostles (1 Cor. 2:9–10; 2
Peter 1:20–21; Hebrews 1:1). These revealed mysteries
are now embodied in the Scriptures and the Christian

preacher is the steward of God who is charged to make them known to the rest of God's household.

The sacred stewardship of the New Testament, however, is a privilege too precious to be confined to preachers and pastors of churches. Every Christian is also a steward of God who has been entrusted with certain goods, not for their own benefit, but for the blessing of the 'household of faith' (Gal. 6:10). Our Lord's parables of the talents and the minas (Matt. 25:14–30; Luke 19:11–27) illustrate the responsibility of every Christian to improve and use the opportunities and gifts that Christ has given to him or her. For God's stewards must neither hoard nor waste the Master's goods that have been committed to their trust. They are to dispense them for the good of the whole of God's household.

Peter brings this concept forward most explicitly. In his memorable words in 1 Peter 4:10 he says, 'As each one has received a gift, minister it to one another (literally, employ it in serving one another), as good stewards of the manifold (literally, 'variegated' or 'many-coloured') grace of God.' As Christians we have all been entrusted with differing gifts to use in the service of one another. Paul says the same thing in Romans 12,

Having then gifts differing according to the grace that is given to us, let us use them: if prophecy, let us prophesy in proportion to our faith; or ministry, let us use it in our ministering (or service); he who teaches, in teaching; he who exhorts, in exhortation; he who gives, with liberality; he who leads, with diligence; he who shows mercy, with cheerfulness (Rom. 12:6–8).

The calling to Christian stewardship

Not everyone can be a steward of God as we have just defined and illustrated from Scripture. It is a divine calling. Again and again God is described in the New Testament as the One who called you (Rom. 8:30; 1 Cor. 1:9; 1 Thess. 4:7, 5:24; 2 Thess. 2:14; 2 Tim. 1:9; 1 Peter 1:15) and Christians as 'the called' (Rom. 8:28). It is a call to the most glorious (1 Cor. 2:9; 2 Thess. 2:13–14; 1 Peter 5:10) and most purposeful and meaningful life on earth imaginable (1 Cor. 1:20–31; Eph. 2:8–10; Phil. 3:7–14; Col. 1:9–10; Titus 2:11–14; 1 Peter 2:9). But it is a call that must be initiated by God in his grace because we are all born into this world as the 'enemies' of God who need to be 'reconciled' to God through the death of his Son (Rom. 5:10; Col. 1:21–22). By nature we are not the servants of God but the 'slaves of sin' (Rom. 6:17), and no human power of will can deliver us from our bias to sin and self. Left to ourselves we will forever go on pleasing the devil and the desires of our flesh. Only God can change our innermost being and set us 'free from sin' to become 'slaves of righteousness' (Rom. 6:18).

To experience this miracle of being spiritually 'born again', as Jesus called it (John 3:3–8), we have to cast ourselves on the mercy of God to give us grace to turn our backs on sin and start following Jesus Christ in a life of devoted service to the glory of God.

By a deliberate and sincere act of faith quickened by God, we have to commit ourselves body and soul to Christ as our Lord and Saviour and put our trust in him to transform our evil heart into a good heart. He alone has the divine power to change us from a child of the devil (John 8:44) into a child of God. This is the promise that we are given in John 1:12: 'to all who received him, who believed in his name, he gave power to become children of God' (RSV). At the moment we become the children of God we enter the household of God where we are appointed as his stewards to serve one another in the cause of advancing his kingdom.

It is tremendously important to understand this. A man can tidy up his old life and try to make it look more religious, but he can never acquire a new one — he cannot buy it, earn it or create it. As Jesus told Nicodemus: 'That which is born of the flesh is flesh, and that which is born of the Spirit is spirit. Do not marvel that I said to you, "You must be born again"' (John 3:6–7). It is something that only God can do, and God can only do it because of what Christ did on the cross to remove the offence of sin that was preventing God from creating in man a clean and steadfast heart (Ps. 51:10). On the cross God dealt with Jesus in accordance with what we deserved as vile sinners, and he now deals with us in accordance

with what Christ deserves as his holy Son in whom he
is well pleased. The sins of believing sinners imputed
to Christ have been paid for and forgiven, and the perfect
obedience of Christ imputed to believing sinners fully
guarantees their acceptance with God and their
appointment as stewards in his household.

THINK ABOUT IT

Seeing we are born God's enemies, we must be new born
his sons.
— *Richard Baxter*

Regeneration is the communication of the divine nature to
man by the operation of the Holy Spirit through the Word.
— *A. J. Gordon*

Regeneration is inseparable from its effects and one of its
effects is God-honouring service.
— *the author*

Have you, dear reader, experienced this divine calling?
Has the Holy Spirit, through the reading and teaching
of holy Scripture, opened your eyes to see the truth in
Jesus and embrace him as the supreme object of your
faith and affections? Has your spirit been regenerated
(born again) and your will freed from self to choose God
and the life of good works that every Christian has been
created in Christ Jesus to walk in (Eph. 2:10)? Unless
you can answer those questions in the affirmative, you

are not a Christian and you are not able to serve God as his faithful steward. You may attempt to do so by trying to do your bit in the church you belong to, but your service of necessity will not be sincere, selfless, enduring, God honouring and God blessed.

I beg you, before you read any further in this book, to answer the call of the Holy Spirit and surrender your life without reserve to Jesus Christ as your Lord and Saviour. Whoever you are, whatever you have done, however long you have delayed, Jesus will receive you and make you a new person (2 Cor. 5:17) whose aim is to be well pleasing to him (2 Cor. 5:9). For he has promised: 'All that the Father gives me will come to me, and the one who comes to me I will by no means cast out' (John 6:37).

The extent of Christian stewardship

Paul tells us in Philippians 2:8–10 that because Jesus Christ 'humbled himself and became obedient to... the death of the cross... God also has highly exalted him and given him the name which is above every name, that at the name of Jesus every knee should bow'. Peter says in Acts 10:36 that 'He is Lord of all'. That is true of all creation, but it is especially true of the Christian. 'You are not your own', says Paul, 'for you were bought at a price; therefore glorify God in your body and in your spirit, which are God's' (1 Cor. 6:19–20). That means that there is not a part of my life or yours as a Christian that does not belong to Jesus Christ and over which he is not Lord. Everything we are and have, both physical and spiritual, is Christ's.

We will be considering what this involves in much greater detail in the ensuing chapters, but it is important at this point to outline the main areas in which we are to be faithful stewards. The obvious place to begin is with the *body*. The body is the vehicle through which every word and deed is expressed. So our hands and our feet, our eyes and our ears, our tongue and our desires and affections must *all* be devoted to the cause of God. To quote Paul again: 'Therefore, whether you eat or drink, or whatever you do, do all to the glory of God' (1 Cor. 10:31).

A second area of stewardship is our *mind*. We are what we think. 'For as he thinks in his heart, so is he', is the warning of Proverbs 23:7. Temptation comes first through the mind, it then kindles our passions and finally gives birth to sin. James says, 'Who is wise and understanding among you? Let him show by good conduct that his works are done in the meekness of wisdom' (James 3:13). That is to say, we should meekly submit our minds to 'the wisdom that is from above' (James 3:17).

A third area of stewardship is the *gifts or abilities* that God has given us. Some have the gift of friendship, some the gift of speaking, some the gift of serving, some the gift of organizing, some the gift of music, and others have the gift of practical skills. We could go on *ad infinitum*, but all these gifts are to be employed for the glory of God, whether at home or at work or at church. The Bible exhorts us: 'Do not neglect the gift that is in you' (1 Tim. 4:14). And again: 'As each one has received a special gift, employ it in serving one another as good stewards of the manifold grace of God' (1 Peter 4:10, NASB).

Fourth, stewardship involves the *use of time*. Time is a precious commodity given to us by God. We are to use time wisely — for his glory and the good of others. If we are not careful and disciplined, we can waste time by pursuing the things of this passing world. As Paul exhorts the Ephesians: 'See then that you walk circumspectly, not as fools but as wise, redeeming the time, because the days are evil' (Eph. 5:15–16). The NASB has 'making the most of your time'.

Fifth, we are called to be 'stewards of the mysteries of God' or the *gospel* (1 Cor. 4:1). Christ has given us the gospel and commissioned us to preach it to every nation. The gospel is a sacred trust, which, until it is passed on to those who do not know it, is like an unpaid debt (Rom. 1:14–15).

Sixth, the Bible speaks of the stewardship of our *wealth*. It is not an accident that seventeen of the thirty-six parables of our Lord had to do with our use of property and possessions. The Bible commands us to 'honour the Lord with [our] possessions' (Prov. 3:9). It is God alone who gives us the health, wisdom, and opportunity to earn riches, and he expects us to use what he has given us to advance his kingdom. David had it right when he brought his offering and that of the people of God for the building of the temple. He said,

> But who am I, and who are my people,
> That we should be able to offer so willingly as this?
> For all things come from you,
> And of your own we have given you (1 Chr. 29:14).

In the seventh place the Bible speaks about the stewardship of our *homes*. This is another of God's good gifts. Proverbs 18:22 says, 'He who finds a wife finds a good thing, and obtains favour from the Lord.' Solomon says, 'Unless the Lord builds the house, they labour in vain who build it... children are a heritage from the Lord, the fruit of the womb is a reward' (Ps. 127:1,3). The writer of Hebrews exhorts, 'Do not forget to entertain strangers, for by so doing some have unwittingly entertained angels' (Heb. 13:2). Peter says, 'Be hospitable to one another without grumbling' (1 Peter 4:9).

In the eighth place, from the beginning Scripture holds us accountable for the management of the *environment*. The world is not here by chance. God created it (Gen. 1:1) and therefore it belongs to him (Ps. 24:1). The earth is his gigantic farm and we are the managers or bailiffs who farm it on his behalf. So the dominion over the earth that God delegated to us in Genesis 1:28 is a responsible dominion. It is a dominion entrusted to us not by right but only by favour. We are accountable to God who has appointed us to take care of the earth and the other creatures that work on it and should benefit from it.

Because this last aspect of stewardship is hotly debated today and the subject of much complex scientific investigation, it would be presumptuous to try and cover the issue in a single chapter, which is all that a book of this size will allow. I will therefore leave it to the reader to pursue this matter at some other time through the many books on ecology that are available. It is, however, important to recognize that all men and women, by virtue of their creation in the image of God, have been entrusted with the care of the environment.

The reward of Christian stewardship

One of the most repeated themes in the teaching of Jesus and his apostles is that God will reward Christians in heaven according to their stewardship on earth. So in the parable of the talents in Matthew 25, the man who had been given five talents and the man who had been given two talents were both rewarded with their master's praise: 'Well done, good and faithful servant; you were faithful over a few things, I will make you ruler over many things. Enter into the joy of your lord' (Matt. 25:21,23). The stewards of God will be rewarded not according to their *successfulness* but according to their *faithfulness*. For as Paul says, 'So then neither he who plants is anything, nor he who waters, but God who gives the increase. Now he who plants and he who waters are one, and each one will receive his own reward according to his own labor (1 Cor. 3:7–8).

That being so, Christians should surely seek to be wise and faithful stewards of all that God has given them, living and longing for the day when they will see Christ's face and receive their eternal reward. It is a demanding life, but as Spurgeon once said, 'If by excessive zeal we die before reaching the average age of man, worn out in the Master's service, then glory to God, we shall have so much less of earth and so much more of heaven.'

This is the glorious service to which every Christian has been called. May God give us grace to respond in the words of Charles Wesley:

> If so poor a worm as I
>   May to Thy glory live;
> All my actions sanctify,
>   All my words and thoughts receive.
> Claim me for Thy service, claim
>   All I have and all I am.

KEY THOUGHTS

Stewardship is a divine calling. Jesus Christ alone has the power to take someone who is a child of the devil and a slave of sin and change him or her into a child of God and a slave of righteousness. In the New Testament God does not have any children who are not also stewards, responsible for dispensing the goods he has entrusted to them for the benefit of the whole household.

QUESTIONS FOR DISCUSSION

1. Every Christian is a steward of God. Substantiate this claim with at least five New Testament references.

2. Read Luke 16:1–13.
   a. List the 'goods' God has entrusted to you.
   b. What accusation was brought against this steward?
   c. Are you guilty of the same charge and in what area or areas?

3. Describe the responsibilities of a steward of God as outlined in Luke 12:42–48, 1 Corinthians 4:2 and 1 Peter 4:10.

4. What encouragements and warnings do Matthew 25:14–30 and 1 Corinthians 3:5–15 give to every Christian?

SUGGESTIONS FOR PRAYER

1. Acknowledge that God is your Master in heaven and thank him for sending his only begotten Son to give his life as a ransom to redeem you from the slavery of sin.

2. *Ask for forgiveness through Christ for all the years you have spent just serving yourself and the devil in opposition to God's purposes. Though your sin is great cast yourself on his grace, which is infinitely greater.*

3. *Pray that for Christ's sake God will help you to faithfully execute your duties in his household to the end of your days.*

Amazing grace! how sweet the sound,
    That saved a wretch like me!
I once was lost, but now am found,
    Was blind, but now I see.

'Twas grace that taught my heart to fear,
    And grace my fears relieved;
How precious did that grace appear,
    The hour I first believed!

Through many dangers, toils and snares,
    I have already come;
'Tis grace has brought me safe thus far,
    And grace will lead me home.

The Lord has promised good to me,
    His word my hope secures;
He will my shield and portion be,
    As long as life endures.

Yes, when this flesh and heart shall fail,
    And mortal life shall cease;
I shall possess, within the veil,
    A life of joy and peace.

The earth shall soon dissolve like snow,
    The sun forbear to shine;
But God, who called me here below,
    Will be for ever mine.

— *John Newton (1725–1807)*

CHAPTER TWO

A STEWARD
UNDER GRACE

BIBLE REFERENCE

And do not present your members as instruments of unrighteousness to sin, but present yourselves to God as being alive from the dead, and your members as instruments of righteousness to God. For sin shall not have dominion over you, for you are not under law but under grace (Rom. 6:13–14).

INTRODUCTION

A Christian, says Paul, is 'not under law but under grace' (Rom. 6:14). To be under God's grace is to have our whole life controlled by grace. Our life is to be accepted, treated, motivated, empowered and governed by grace. Christian stewardship, therefore, is not a service imposed on us but a service that is freely, wholeheartedly and joyfully given in response to the grace that God has lavished on us in Christ. Redeemed undeservedly by God at infinite cost, our supreme desire is to live 'to the praise of the glory of his grace' (Eph. 1:6).

Grace is what Christianity is all about. The gospel contains both an announcement and a summons. The announcement is that grace has come to sinners in and through Jesus Christ (Rom. 5:15–17). The summons is God's command that sinners receive this grace (2 Cor. 6:1) and continue in it (Acts 13:43) because 'the word of his grace… is able to build you up and give you an inheritance among all those who are sanctified' (Acts 20:32).

The meaning of grace

The Greek word for grace is *charis* and its basic meaning is that of a free and undeserved gift. It is something given to a man or woman, unearned and unmerited, by the sheer generosity of God's love. Romans 6:23 is a good example of the essential meaning of the word. There the 'wages of sin' and 'the gift of God' are contrasted with each other. The word translated as wages is *opsonia*, and it was the common word used to refer to a soldier's pay. So the pay we earn for serving sin is death. In stark contrast, however, 'the *charisma* of God is eternal life'. It is unearned and freely given out of the goodness of God's heart through our Lord Jesus Christ.

This was the essence of the preaching of the apostles. In Acts 15:11 Peter says, 'We believe that through the grace [*charitos*] of the Lord Jesus Christ we shall be saved.' That is to say, we are saved through the undeserved favour and unmerited love of Jesus who of his own free will took the initiative to empty himself of his heavenly glory to become our servant and 'give his life a ransom for many' (Mark 10:45). He did it all in grace for he was in no way obliged to show mercy to sinners who hate him without a cause (John 15:23–25) and deserve nothing more than to be condemned to everlasting punishment in hell (Matt. 25:46). His love for us depends *only* on his own will. God was free to *not* be gracious to sinners.

So to state that we are saved 'through the grace of the Lord Jesus Christ' (Acts 15:11) is another way of saying that we are not saved (not even in a little way) by our-selves. It is all of God in Christ acting in spontaneous, undeserved goodness to save sinners; God loving the unlovely, revealing himself to them, moving them to respond to him, pardoning their sins, adopting them as his own children, and overcoming every obstacle in the way of bringing them ultimately into full fellowship and enjoyment of himself in glory.

To the apostles of Jesus Christ, grace is an incomparable wonder. They cannot find sufficient words to describe it. Indeed, Paul calls it an 'indescribable gift' (2 Cor. 9:15). Elsewhere he speaks of 'the exceeding riches of his grace in his kindness toward us in Christ Jesus' (Eph. 2:7) and of 'the unsearchable riches of Christ' (Eph. 3:8). Given man's depravity and sin before God, the apostles are absolutely flabbergasted that God should love us so much as to willingly suffer the pangs of hell in order to save us from such a fate.

The great hymnwriters of the church have also been enraptured by the wonder of God's grace. They speak of 'Amazing grace, how sweet the sound, that saved a wretch like me!' and 'Marvelous grace of our loving Lord, grace that exceeds our sin and our guilt'; and again, 'Amazing love! How can it be, that Thou, my God, should'st die for me?' And yet again, 'Wonderful the matchless grace of Jesus... how shall my tongue describe it?' They are overwhelmed by the fact that God was willing to be gracious even to the point of taking on himself the just punishment due to man's lawbreaking (2 Cor. 5:19).

Samuel Davies, in his lovely hymn, sees God's grace shining with unrivalled glory among all of God's wondrous acts:

Great God of wonders! all Thy ways
    Display Thy attributes divine;
But countless acts of pardoning grace
    Beyond Thine other wonders shine:
Who is a pardoning God like Thee?
    Or who has grace so rich and free?

In wonder lost, with trembling joy
    We take the pardon of our God;
Pardon for crimes of deepest dye,
    A pardon, bought with Jesus' blood:
Who is a pardoning God like Thee?
    Or who has grace so rich and free?

O may this strange, this matchless grace,
    This God-like miracle of love,
Fill the wide earth with grateful praise,
    As now it fills the choirs above!
Who is a pardoning God like Thee?
    Or who has grace so rich and free?

THINK ABOUT IT

Grace in God is his compassion on the unworthy.
— *Andrew Murray*

48

THINK ABOUT IT

Grace is what all need, what none can merit and what God alone can give.
— *George Barlow*

The grace of God... is a much higher thing than the grace of a king to his dutiful subjects; it has its inspiration not in the worthiness of those to whom it is shown, but entirely in the heart of God himself.
— *Ernest F. Kevan*

EXPLANATION

The sufficiency of grace

By nature all human beings are 'slaves of sin' (Rom. 6:17) and 'without strength' (Rom. 5:6) to save themselves from such terrible bondage. It is only by grace — by the merciful, sovereign and omnipotent intervention of God — that sinners can be saved (Eph. 2:4–10). Men and women in their fallen condition have neither the desire nor the ability to come to God in repentance and faith. Repentance and faith are gifts that have to be given by God's grace if sinners are going to be able to turn from their sin and put their trust in Jesus Christ — to save them from sin's penalty, power and presence.

First, let us consider repentance. Peter says, 'Him [Jesus] God has exalted to his right hand to be Prince and Saviour, to give repentance to Israel and forgiveness of sins' (Acts 5:31). Again, when Peter told his fellow apostles how a Roman

centurion and his household were surprisingly converted, 'they glorified God, saying, "Then God has also
granted to the Gentiles repentance to life"' (Acts 11:18).
Repentance is the gift of God.

But the desire to believe in Christ and commit one's
life to him is also the gift of God's grace according to
the New Testament. So Paul writes, 'For by grace you
have been saved through faith, and that not of yourselves; it is the gift of God, not of works, lest anyone
should boast' (Eph. 2:8–9). Now whether 'it' refers to
just faith or to the whole experience of salvation
through faith, does not matter; whatever view you
take, Paul is still saying that faith is the gift of God.
The context makes it clear that faith is only possible
because we who are dead in trespasses have been
raised with Christ to spiritual life and given the power
to believe. As Paul wrote earlier: 'But God, who is rich
in mercy, because of his great love with which he
loved us, even when we were dead in trespasses, made
us alive together with Christ (by grace you have been
saved), and raised us up together' (Eph. 2:4–6).
Elsewhere, Luke says that Paul 'greatly helped those
who had believed through grace' (Acts 18:27).

God's work of grace in the Christian, however, does
not stop at conversion. God's grace is a love that *saves*
and a love that *keeps*. Thus God in his grace also takes
the initiative to preserve in Christ those whom he has
united to his Son by faith through the Holy Spirit. For
example, Peter speaks of Christians as those 'who are
kept by the power of God through faith for salvation
ready to be revealed in the last time' (1 Peter 1:5). Paul

shares the same confidence with his converts: 'He who has begun a good work in you will complete it until the day of Jesus Christ' (Phil. 1:6). To Timothy, Paul writes, 'I know whom I have believed and am persuaded that he is able to keep what I have committed to him until that Day.' And again, 'The Lord will deliver me from every evil work and preserve me for his heavenly kingdom' (2 Tim. 1:12; 4:18). But clearest of all is the promise of our Saviour himself: 'My sheep hear my voice, and I know them, and they follow me. And I give them eternal life, and they shall never perish; neither shall anyone snatch them out of my hand' (John 10:27–28).

From start to finish salvation is a work of divine, all-sufficient grace. Where grace is present it reigns (Rom. 5:21) and nothing can stop it from fulfilling God's purpose in the life of every one of his elect. Augustus Toplady, who is the poet of Christian assurance, sums it up like this:

A sovereign protector I have,
    Unseen, yet for ever at hand,
Unchangeably faithful to save,
    Almighty to rule and command.
He smiles and my comforts abound;
    His grace as the dew shall descend
And walls of salvation surround
    The soul He delights to defend.

THINK ABOUT IT

They have no grace that can be content with a little grace.
— *Thomas Manton*

God's grace is not only amazing grace, it is abounding grace.
— *Vance Havner*

It is a greater work of God to bring men to grace than, being in the state of grace, to bring them to glory; because sin is far more distant from grace than grace is from glory.
— *John Trapp*

The relation between grace and law

Christians are called to a life of good works. Paul writes, 'For we are his workmanship, created in Christ Jesus for good works, which God prepared beforehand that we should walk in them' (Eph. 2:10). Christians are to 'be rich in good works' (1 Tim. 6:18; see also 2 Tim. 3:17; Titus 2:7,14; 3:8,14). And a good work in the New Testament is one that is done according to God's revealed will in Scripture, out of love to God and our neighbour, and with the supreme purpose of glorifying our Father in heaven (Matt. 5:16).

Professing Christians can go wrong in two ways regarding the practice of good works. In the first place they can fall prey to *legalism*, which is a form of pride. Legalists do their good works with the wrong motive and purpose because they view them as a way to earn more of God's favour than they presently enjoy. They need to feel that they can contribute something to their acceptance with God. A non-contributory scheme of salvation does not appeal to them at all. This is a natural, fallen reaction to God's grace. We do not like to be treated as paupers who depend *entirely* on the charity of heaven. We do not want to be totally indebted to God the Son. We say, 'Please Jesus, let me contribute something. Let me feel that I have had a tiny share in being made acceptable to you. Do not humiliate me by making me look so useless.' But Jesus will not have it! We deserve nothing so we can contribute nothing. To quote William Temple: 'The only thing of my very own which I contribute to my redemption, is the sin from which I need to be redeemed.' That is all. We have nothing else to contribute. God in Christ, as we have already seen, does it all.

Despite this, throughout the history of the gospel, men and women have rebelled in pride against the grace of God. Thus in the churches of Galatia the Judaizers said, 'Well, the work of Jesus is fine! But you still have to be circum-cised; you still have to add to the work of Jesus some work of your own, if you are going to find acceptance with God' (Gal. 2–3, *author's paraphrase*). And in the church at Colosse there were those who said that Christians needed some secret philosophy plus Jesus to attain spiritual completion. But Paul condemned both of these 'Christ-plus' teachings as false gospels that obscured and denied the all-sufficiency of the grace of God revealed in Jesus: 'Indeed I, Paul, say to you that if you become circumcised, Christ will profit you nothing... you have become estranged from Christ, you who attempt to be justified by law; you have fallen from grace' (Gal. 5:2,4). And again, 'Beware lest anyone cheat you through philosophy and empty deceit... For in him [Christ] dwells all the fulness of the Godhead bodily; and you are complete in him' (Col. 2:8–10).

Modern religionists make the same mistake. They want the salvation of their soul to be a joint enterprise. 'God helps those who help themselves', they say. You have a part to play in improving your status with God. For some, this means receiving Holy Communion every week from the hand of a priest who has been ordained by bishops in the apostolic succession. Others affirm that you have to be baptized before God will truly accept you. And still others say that you have to speak in tongues, otherwise you are not completely saved. And so the lamentable list of contributory works of salvation goes on: you must stop smoking and drinking, you must go to church twice every Sunday, you must speak of Christ to at least one person every day, you must tithe all your income, and so on. There is no end to it! But in essence they are all the same. They are proclaiming a 'Christ-plus' way of earning more accept-ance with God than what Christ has already won for us. This reversion to legalism dishonours Christ and frustrates grace (Gal. 2:21, AV).

So, far from increasing our favour with God, as it claims to do, legalism in all its forms does the very opposite. It alienates us from Christ because everyone who believes that they can improve their relationship with God by their own religious good works is effectively saying that they do not trust Jesus exclusively. All that Jesus has done for a world of sinners is not enough. There is only one word for that: apostasy. Such people have fallen from grace. Justification has to be by faith alone in Christ alone because Christ alone has satisfied all the demands of God's law. If your aim is to satisfy God by obeying the rules, you have to submit to every single one of them. As Paul argues in Galatians 3:10, a fifty per cent mark will not suffice to pass God's moral examination. He demands 100 per cent obedience, 100 per cent of the time. Only fools believe that they can attain such an impossible standard. Legalistic religion in all its forms should be shunned and guarded against because it starves our souls to feed our pride.

Antinomianism, which means being 'anti-law', goes to the other extreme. It denies that God's moral law in Scripture (his revealed will) should determine the practice of good works for which Christians have been created in Christ Jesus. Freedom from the moral law as a way of salvation is said to bring with it freedom from the law as a code for Christian behaviour. And so whereas legalists magnify the law by minimizing grace, antinomians magnify grace by minimizing the law. God, they argue, sees no sin in believers because Christ's perfect law-keeping has been imputed to them, and therefore their daily conduct is inconsequential as long as they keep trusting in Christ. But 1 John 1:8–2:1 and 3:4–10 make it perfectly clear that it is not possible to be 'in Christ' and at the same time to be unconcerned about repeated sin and disobedience in our life.

Keeping God's moral law as revealed in Scripture is the continuing obligation of every Christian (Rom. 3:31). 'I am not free from God's law but am under Christ's law', says Paul (1 Cor. 9:21, NIV). In addition, the Christian is called to a life of daily repentance in which he or she continually seeks God's help in keeping his law. Indeed, the Holy Spirit has been given to us to write God's moral law on our hearts (Jer. 31:33) and cause us to walk in his statutes (Ezek. 36:26–27). Scripture gives no assurance of salvation to any who claim to believe in Christ but do not seek to turn from their idols to serve the living and true God in works of righteousness (1 Cor. 6:9–11; 1 Thess. 1:9; Rev. 21:8).

Instead of giving us an excuse to break God's law, grace upholds the moral law as a rule of conduct for the Christian. 'For the grace of God that brings salvation', writes Paul, 'has appeared to all men, teaching us that, denying ungodliness and worldly lusts, we should live soberly, righteously and godly in the present age' (Titus 2:11–12). What could be plainer than that? The New Testament doctrine of free and sovereign grace both humbles the pride of the legalist and condemns the self-indulgence of the antinomian. It transforms the good works we ought to do but naturally are not inclined to do, into service that we delight to do because we love 'the God of all grace' who has redeemed us at such infinite cost to himself (1 Peter 1:15–19; 5:10).

The freedom of grace

EXPLANATION

To live not under law but under grace is to know true freedom. This is what our Lord Jesus Christ promised his disciples when he said, 'Therefore if the Son makes you free, you shall be free indeed' (John 8:36). Christians under grace are free, in the first place, from *the condemnation of the law* (Rom. 8:1–2). They are no longer oppressed by the awful burden of trying to earn acceptance with God by perfectly satisfying the demands of God's moral law. Saved by grace, they live with the assurance that they are eternally forgiven and cannot lose their salvation even when they fail God — and they will fail because of the remaining sin in their lives. However, when they fail, they do not capitulate. Instead, they pick themselves up and seek God's pardon and grace to go on in their Christian lives.

Second, Christians under grace are free from *the control of sin*. To the Christians in Rome Paul writes, 'For sin shall not have dominion over you, for you are not under law but under grace' (Rom. 6:14). No Christian can enjoy sinning as he or she did before their conversion, because their union by faith with Christ crucified and risen has changed their nature. 'Therefore, if anyone is in Christ, he is a new creation; old things have passed away; behold, all things have become new' (2 Cor. 5:17). And whereas before their conversion they sought only to please themselves, they now make it their aim to be well pleasing to God (2 Cor. 5:9).

Here is how Paul puts it in Romans 7:21–25:

> I find then a law, that evil is present with me, the one who wills to do good. For I delight in the law of God according to the inward man. But I see another law in my members, warring against the law of my mind, and bringing me into captivity to the law of sin which is in my members. O wretched man that I am! Who will deliver me from this body of death? I thank God — through Jesus Christ our Lord!
>
> So then, with the mind I myself serve the law of God, but with the flesh the law of sin.

The Christian life is a battle with sin but because of God's grace in conversion Christians possess both the desire and the strength to do God's will — and it is only as they do so that they will be happy and fulfilled.

Third, the Christian under grace is free from *the intimidation of adverse circumstances* (Rom. 8:28–39). It may be the threat of 'distress, or persecution, or famine, or nakedness, or peril, or sword' but the Christian is not intimidated because he or she knows that they belong

EXPLANATION

to Christ and nothing can separate them from the love of God that is in Christ Jesus their Lord. The Christian knows that 'all things work together for good to those who love God, to those who are the called according to his purpose'. So when fear grips the soul of a Christian, as it will from time to time, he or she will know what to do — they will bolster their faith by reminding themselves of the fact that if God is for them, who can be against them?

The motivation of grace

Rightly understood, the doctrine of God's free and sovereign grace also promotes tireless energy for 'good works, which God prepared beforehand that we should walk in them' (Eph. 2:10). For if Christian doctrine is about grace, Christian duty is about gratitude. As John says, 'We love him because he first loved us' (1 John 4:15). If Christians today knew more about God's grace, the world would see much more godly service than it does. The greatness of the self-sacrificing love of Christ in suffering the God-forsaken death of the cross that our sins rightly deserved should drive us to give ourselves in devoted abandonment to advance his kingdom. Any person who claims to be a Christian and yet is not full of gratitude and motivated to spend their life on God has a reason to wonder if he or she is really saved.

The transforming effect of God's grace in the life of a Christian is graphically illustrated in the dynamic change that came over Saul of Tarsus — a persecutor of the church who later became the apostle to the Gentiles. He writes, 'But by the grace of God I am what I am, and his grace toward me was not in vain; but I labored more abundantly than they all, yet not I, but the grace of God which was with me' (1 Cor. 15:10). This verse indicates that the man now known as Paul attributed not only his conversion to God's grace but also all that he was able to do and achieve throughout the course of his life and ministry as an apostle.

It is therefore significant that the word that Paul and the other apostles loved to use more than any other to describe their relationship to their Saviour was *doulos* — it literally means a 'slave or bondservant of Jesus Christ' (Rom. 1:1). It is a very strong word suggesting nothing less than complete and utter bondage — yet in the New Testament it means a bondage that is spontaneous, voluntary, joyful and wholehearted.

What is more, this service is rendered not with the hope of receiving something but in *response* to something already received. 'For the love of Christ compels us', says Paul (2 Cor. 5:14). All of a Christian's service is to be offered in the light of the amazing love of the one who, as Paul says in the next verse, 'died for all, that those who live should live no longer for themselves, but for him who died for them and rose again' (2 Cor. 5:15).

This concept of a Christian being the devoted bond-servant of Jesus Christ is almost certainly derived from the law governing Hebrew slaves in Exodus 21. There we read:

> If you buy a Hebrew servant, he shall serve six years; and in the seventh he shall go out free and pay nothing. If he comes in by himself, he shall go out by himself; if he comes in married, then his wife shall go out with him. If his master has given him a wife, and she has borne him sons or daughters, the wife and her children shall be her master's, and he shall go out by himself. But if the servant plainly says, 'I love my master, my wife, and my children; I will not go out free,' then his master shall bring him to the judges. He shall also bring him to the door, or to the doorpost, and his master shall pierce his ear with an awl; and he shall serve him forever (Exod. 21:2–6).

It is the same principle: the Hebrew slave has served his time and by a decree of God's grace must be set free. However, if he loves his master because he is a good master who has given him a wife and children, he may follow the instincts of his heart and bind himself to serve his master joyfully and devotedly for the rest of his life.

The prodigal son in Jesus' parable felt a similar devotion. When this sinner came to his senses in a far country and saw how harmful and how hurtful to his father his lust for selfish pleasures had been he said, 'I will arise and go to my father, and will say to him, "Father, I have sinned against heaven and before you, and am no longer worthy to be called your son. Make me like one of your hired servants"' (Luke 15:18). That is all that the prodigal son hoped for. If only his father would forgive his wanton and wasteful life, he would spend his remaining days gratefully serving in his father's household. And that is precisely the sentiment of every truly repentant sinner before God. We know that we deserve only God's eternal wrath, but if he can find it in his heart of mercy to forgive us through Christ, we will love and serve him for ever.

Is this not also how the sinful woman in Luke 7 felt? Christ had forgiven her sins, which were many, and so she disregarded the criticism and the disdain of the religious authorities who sat at the table with Jesus in the house of Simon the Pharisee. Driven by grateful love, she washed the Saviour's feet with her tears, dried them with her hair, kissed them and then anointed them with costly fragrant oil. It was a courageous and sacrificial act of worship. And when Christ was criticized for accepting her grateful, loving service, he replied, 'Her sins, which are many, are forgiven, for she loved much. But to whom little is forgiven, the same loves little' (Luke 7:50). The one who loves and serves God most will be the person who is most conscious of the love God has shown to him in Christ. To quote Robert Trail: 'When you have kindled your love to Christ at his love for you, then let it burn and spend... in his service and to his praise.'

KEY THOUGHTS

KEY THOUGHTS

In all the Word of God there is no doctrine which, if properly applied, is more conducive to godly living than is the doctrine of salvation by grace, and by grace alone.
— *R. B. Kuiper*

Oh! To grace how great a debtor
　　Daily I'm constrained to be;
Let that grace now, like a fetter,
　　Bind my wandering heart to Thee.
— *Robert Robinson*

How strange that the Lord must plead with those whom he has saved from the pit to show gratitude to him!
— *Donald Grey Barnhouse*

QUESTIONS FOR DISCUSSION

DISCUSS IT

1. *Explain the nature and measure of God's grace, and give references from the New Testament to substantiate your statements.*

2. *Read Romans 6:1–23 and draw out of Paul's teaching the implications of being 'under grace'.*

3. *What are the dangers of legalism and antinomianism*

to Christian living? See Galatians 5:2–4; Colossians 2:8–10; Romans 6:1–4; Titus 2:11–12; 1 John 1:8–2:1; 3:4–10.

4. In what way does grace bring freedom to a Christian's life? See Romans 8:1–2; 6:14; 7:21–25; 8:28–39.

5. Give three New Testament passages that speak of grace promoting tireless energy in the service of God. Is this proving true in your life?

SUGGESTIONS FOR PRAYER

1. If you are a Christian thank the God of all grace that he turned you from idols to serve him, the living and true God. Ask him by his Holy Spirit to constrain you more and more by his grace to serve him better.

2. If you are not a Christian, ask God to be merciful to you, a sinner, and give you grace to turn from your sins in repentance and receive the Lord Jesus Christ by faith as your personal Saviour. Then, like Saul of Tarsus, ask the Lord to show you what service he wants you to do (Acts 9:6).

Take my life, and let it be
    Consecrated, Lord, to Thee;
Take my moments and my days,
    Let them flow in ceaseless praise.

Take my hands, and let them move
    At the impulse of Thy love;
Take my feet, and let them be
    Swift and 'beautiful' for Thee.

Take my voice, and let me sing
    Always, only, for my King;
Take my lips, and let them be
    Filled with messages from Thee.

Take my silver and my gold;
    Not a mite would I withhold;
Take my intellect, and use
    Every power as Thou shalt choose.

Take my will, and make it Thine;
    It shall be no longer mine;
Take my heart, it is Thine own;
    It shall be Thy royal throne.

Take my love; my Lord, I pour
    At Thy feet its treasure-store;
Take myself, and I will be
    Ever, only, all for Thee.

— Frances Ridley Havergal (1836–1879)

CHAPTER THREE

THE
STEWARDSHIP
OF OUR
BODY

LOOK IT UP

BIBLE REFERENCE

I beseech you therefore, brethren,
by the mercies of God, that you present your bodies
a living sacrifice, holy, acceptable to God,
which is your reasonable service
(Rom. 12:1)

INTRODUCTION

Stewardship is a key aspect of Christian disciple-ship in which we all need to learn and grow. We can very easily become slack and indolent in our service of God. It is our Master's desire that all of his followers should have a deeper understanding of and a greater commitment to their calling as God's stewards.

Now the place to begin, obviously, is with our-selves: with our bodies and our minds. The biblical order is that we must first give *ourselves* to the Lord before we begin to give him our time, abilities, money, home and witness. We will never be faithful in the dedication of the things we value to God until we have first dedicated ourselves to God.

This dedicated service is what endeared the churches of Macedonia to the apostle Paul. He had asked these Christians to contribute to a special famine relief fund that he was organizing for some Christians in Judea. And, although the Macedonian Christians were going through 'a great trial of affliction' and 'deep poverty', Paul says in 2 Corinthians 8:2–5 that they gave 'beyond their ability, they were freely willing, imploring us with much urgency that we would receive the gift and the fellowship of the ministering to the saints'. And this they did, he says, 'not as we had hoped, but [they] first gave themselves to the Lord, and then to us by the will of God'.

Faithful stewardship to God must begin with ourselves. Strange as it may seem, it is possible to be a Christian and yet not be a fully dedicated Christian. It is possible to remain 'a babe in Christ' for much longer than necessary (1 Cor. 3:1–3; Heb. 5:12–14). It is possible to live a life in which Christ has a *place*, maybe even some *prominence*, but he does not have *pre-eminence*. He does not come first in all of our desiring and doing. Hence Paul writes in Romans 12:1 to those who have been Christians for some years and he calls for the *total* consecration of their lives to God: 'I beseech you therefore, brethren, by the mercies of God, that you present your bodies a living sacrifice, holy, acceptable to God, which is your reasonable service.'

The appeal to present our bodies to God

Paul says, 'I beseech you therefore, brethren… that you present your bodies… to God.' This appeal is addressed to all of the Christians in the church at Rome — consisting of Jews and Gentiles, men and women, young and old. Paul describes them as 'brethren' — they were his

EXPLANATION

brothers and sisters in the international family of God. Although Paul had never visited Rome, he knew a number of the believers in the church there from working with them in other cities. In chapter 16 he speaks of them as those who had laboured much in the Lord (Rom. 16:6,12). And yet even these believers are commanded to present their bodies to the Lord, along with the others who Paul did not know personally.

There is an important point to be made here: Christian consecration does not end at the beginning of the Christian life. Our Christian life begins with an act of personal commitment to Jesus Christ when we come to him in penitence and faith and invite him to be our Saviour and Lord. But that indispensable beginning is not the end. We are urged by the apostle to *continually* present our bodies as living sacrifices to God and his service.

In this sense, as the Bible so often asserts, the Christian life resembles marriage. Marriage begins with a decisive commitment of two people to one another, sealed and confessed in a public ceremony. But after that decisive commitment to one another there must be a lifetime of ongoing recommitment to one another in mutual love and self-giving. The initial moment of commitment leads to a lifetime of growing service to one another. And what is true in marriage is equally true in the Christian life. When we come to Christ in repentance and faith we cannot escape committing ourselves to him and his service.

But that moment of commitment must be followed by a
lifetime of adjustment in which we keep presenting our
bodies to Christ and become more and more involved
in his service.

We now focus our attention on the word 'body'. To
the Greeks reading Paul's words, this command to present
their bodies to God would have seemed absurd. Since
they were raised in the philosophy of Plato, they
regarded the body as an embarrassing encumbrance.
The great slogan of the Greeks was that 'the body is a
tomb' and they longed more than anything else for the
release of their spirit from the tomb of their body. So
the idea that we should present our bodies to God as a
living sacrifice would have been utterly abhorrent to
the Greeks. It is also frowned on today by followers of
the mystic religions of the East. Even some Christian
people regard their bodies as a necessary evil. Malcolm
Muggeridge used to often speak of dragging his corpse
around with him.

But this is not how a Christian ought to think about
his or her body. Some of us are told that we have to
give our hearts to Jesus, and we think of having some
kind of mystical experience with Christ from which
our body is excluded. But that is a very erroneous
notion. Paul says that we are first of all to present our
bodies to God. Moreover, he goes on to say that to do
so is not the unspiritual thing that it may seem to be,
for he calls it our 'reasonable' (or spiritual) 'service' (or
worship). It is an interesting paradox. The apostle,
however, is clearly stating that no offering of ourselves
to God can be pleasing to him if it is merely inward

and spiritual. It must express itself in the concrete activities of our bodies, for human beings are a body-soul entity.

Surely no one will argue with that. Our spirit and our mind cannot do anything on earth without our body. Whether we are a saint or sinner, Christian or non-Christian, our body is the vehicle through which we express our personality. When Aaron and his sons were consecrated to the work of the priesthood we read in Leviticus 8:22–24 that Moses killed 'the ram of consecration' and then 'took some of its blood and put it on... the tips of their right ears, on the thumbs of their right hands, and on the big toes of their right feet'. What did that mean? It signified that, from that moment, their hearing was consecrated to the Word of God, their hands were to be used in the work of God and their feet were to walk in the way of God. They were not their own. The blood of sacrifice had consecrated their bodies to the priesthood of God. And that is exactly the claim of the atoning blood of God the Son on us.

It is also interesting that in Romans 3, when Paul is describing the human condition without God, he deliberately refers to different parts of the human body as being in rebellion against God. Paul says,

Their throat is an open tomb;
With their tongues they have practiced
    deceit;

> The poison of asps is under their lips;
> Whose mouth is full of cursing and bitterness.
> Their feet are swift to shed blood...
> There is no fear of God before their eyes
> (Rom. 3:13–18).

In our pre-conversion days these different parts of our body were used in the service of the devil. But now, Paul says, 'do not present your members [the different parts of your bodies] as instruments of unrighteousness to sin, but present yourselves to God as being alive from the dead, and your members as instruments of righteousness to God' (Rom. 6:13; see also 6:16,19).

Christian consecration must be evident in the deeds of our bodies. How gracious of God in salvation to restore our bodies to such noble use! As his servants our lips can speak the truth and spread the gospel. Our tongues can bring encouragement to the fainthearted and healing to those who have been hurt in life. Our hands can lift up those who have fallen, nurse the sick, cook food and clean house for the disabled and perform many other mundane tasks like mending, typing, writing, cutting grass and so on. Our arms can embrace the lonely and unloved with affection. Our ears can listen to the cries of the distressed, the thanksgiving of the blessed and the questions of those who are perplexed or seeking after God. Our eyes can look with compassion on the lost who are like sheep without a shepherd; they can look out for areas of need or ways to improve our service for God; they can look humbly and patiently for God to fulfil his promises and purposes.

In Hebrews 10:5–7 the Spirit of Jesus says, 'Sacrifice and offering you did not desire, but a body you have prepared for me... Then I said, "Behold, I have come... to do your will, O God"' (see also Ps. 40). In order to do the will of God the Father on earth, Jesus had to have a human body. Everything he did to serve God and win salvation for his people, he did through his body. His feet carried him to the towns and villages of Palestine. His hands healed the sick; his lips spoke the words of life; his ears heard the cries of the needy; his eyes wept for the perishing. And at last when he came to Jerusalem to lay down his life for his sheep, Peter says that he 'bore our sins in his own body on the tree' (1 Peter 2:24).

Jesus Christ was the perfect 'Servant' of God (Isa. 49:3–6; 52:13–53:12). And just as he could only accomplish the work of our salvation in his body, so we are called as his servants to express the news and the fruit of that salvation in our bodies today.

In 1 Corinthians 6:15–20 Paul says, 'Do you not know that your bodies are members of Christ? ... Do you not know that your body is the temple of the Holy Spirit who is in you, whom you have from God, and you are not your own? For you were bought at a price; therefore glorify God in your body and in your spirit, which are God's.' This is a serious matter. For what we do with our bodies in this life will determine our reward or loss in the next life. 'For we must all appear before the judgment seat of Christ, so that each one may be recompensed for his deeds in the body, according to what he has done, whether good or bad' (2 Cor. 5:10, NASB).

The manner in which our bodies are to be presented to God

Paul writes, 'I beseech you therefore, brethren... that you present your bodies a living sacrifice, holy, acceptable to God' (Rom. 12:1). There are at least three things in this statement that should characterize the giving of our body in the service of God.

1. It should be decisive

This is implied by the verb 'to present', which is an aorist active infinitive, meaning an action that is done once for all and is not to be revoked. It is the word used of Mary and Joseph presenting the child Jesus to God in the temple and of Christ one day presenting to himself his glorified, unblemished Church. Ideally this full surrender to the service of God should come at our conversion. It did for the apostle Paul on the road to Damascus. The moment he realized that it was Jesus who was confronting him in the blinding brightness of his resurrection glory, his response was: 'Lord, what do you want me to do?' (Acts 9:6). That was a decisive, irrevocable surrender of Paul's life to the service of Christ right at the beginning of his Christian life. It was conclusive. There were no ifs or buts. His commitment was absolute and unconditional.

Often, however, this kind of commitment comes sometime after our conversion when we have gained a clearer understanding of God's will for our lives. The history of the church is replete with the biographies of men and women who later in their Christian life solemnly and decisively handed their lives over to God for his service. Consider the great eighteenth century New England evangelist, Jonathan Edwards. After he had entered into such a transaction with God, he wrote in his diary these words,

I have this day been before God and have given myself, all that I have and am, to God; so that I am in no respect my own. I can no longer challenge any right in myself, in this understanding, this will, these affections. Neither have I the right to this body, or any of its members. No right to this tongue, these hands, these feet, these eyes, these ears. I have given myself clean away.

In a similar vein Philip Henry, the father of the great commentator Matthew Henry, taught his children when they came to faith in Jesus Christ to pray these words of commitment:

I take God the Father to be my God;
I take God the Son to be my Saviour;
I take the Holy Ghost to be my Sanctifier;
I take the Word of God to be my rule;

I take the people of God to be my people;
And I do hereby dedicate and yield my whole self
  to the Lord:
And I do this deliberately, freely and forever.
  Amen.

Consecration is resolution that is not afraid of sacrifice. Heathen devotees can often put us to shame. A missionary who was watching the construction of a beautiful temple asked an Indian woman who was standing nearby, 'How much will it cost?' 'It is for the gods', she replied, 'We do not ask, what will it cost?' Are you holding back because of the fear of what it might cost? God demands that your whole being be placed entirely at his disposal. Do it now. Say in the words of Antoinette Bourignon,

Henceforth may no profane delight
    Divide this consecrated soul;
Possess it Thou, who hast the right,
    As Lord and Master of the whole.

This simple act of presentation, of self-surrender, is what the apostle Paul is appealing for, but it must be decisive and conclusive like the commitment we make to our spouse in marriage. There can be no reservation, no going back, no revocation.

2. It should be a lifelong commitment
Paul draws a contrast here between the dead blood-sacrifices of the Old Testament and the *living* sacrifices of the New. A dead sacrifice is a momentary sacrifice.

When it is over, it is done with — it cannot be re-offered. Sometime later another, separate sacrifice has to be made. That was the sacrifice and service that marked God's people in the Old Testament. But in the New Testament a Christian's sacrifice and service to God is different. It is a continual, lifelong sacrifice.

Christian consecration and service is not just the sacrifice of one day in seven to go to church or the sacrifice of luxuries at Lent. No, it is something much more fundamental than that. It is much easier to make a sacrifice for God from time to time than to do what Paul is entreating us to do here: to give our body as a living sacrifice to God. But that is what is expected of us. The life of a true steward of God in the household of faith is one of perpetual sacrifice. We are bondslaves. We are on call twenty-four hours every day. Our Lord himself required this of all his disciples. He said to them, 'If anyone desires to come after me, let him deny himself, and take up his cross daily, and follow me' (Luke 9:23). Paul accepted this and was able to say to the Corinthians, 'I die daily' (1 Cor. 15:31). He renounced living for himself every day so that he might live for God. He repeatedly calls himself 'a bondslave of Christ' (Rom. 1:1; Gal. 1:10; Titus 1:1).

In one of his books Stephen Olford tells of a young lady who came to him at the close of a meeting and said, 'All this talk about full surrender is

sheer nonsense! It doesn't work.' Dr. Olford saw at once
that she needed a strong word. 'Young lady', he replied,
'you are not really being honest. For it is quite obvious
you have never fully yielded your life to Christ.' Rather
shaken she asked him what he meant. 'Well', he said,
'New Testament surrender is not a matter of a day or a
week, or a year. It is a contract for life. If you say you
have surrendered your life to God, what are you doing
off the altar?' That is it precisely. The consecration of
our bodies to God is to be a living, ongoing sacrifice to
him. But Paul does not stop there when he speaks about
the presentation of our bodies to God.

3. It should also be holy and acceptable to God
Continuing to draw from the service of God in the Old
Testament, Paul exhorts the Romans 'to present your
bodies a living sacrifice, holy, acceptable to God'. Before
a sacrifice could be offered in the Old Testament the
animal had to be brought to the priest and examined for
blemishes. There were twenty blemishes for which
the priest had to look. And only when the priest was
satisfied that the animal was free from blemish, did he
allow it to be offered in sacrifice to God.

Now, mercifully, we are not required to be free from
blemish. If we had to wait until our bodies were sinless,
none of us could ever be used in the service of God. It
is part of God's great condescension that he uses us in
spite of our unworthiness and sinfulness. But that does
not mean that we can be careless about the way we live.
The bodies we are to offer in the service of God must be
holy and acceptable. That is to say there must be no sin

EXPLANATION

that is not repented of in our lives. Our bodies and our souls must be continually cleansed by the merits of the precious blood of our Lord Jesus Christ and by the daily washing of God's Word (1 John 1:7; Eph. 5:26).

Just as a good cook will only use clean vessels and a good surgeon will only use sterilized instruments, so God will only use 'instruments of righteousness' according to Paul in Romans 6:13. In 2 Timothy 2:19–22 Paul is even more blunt. He says, 'Let everyone who names the name of Christ depart from iniquity... If anyone cleanses himself from [iniquity], he will be a vessel for honour, sanctified and useful for the Master, prepared for every good work. Flee also youthful lusts; but pursue righteousness.' The godly Robert Murray M'Cheyne is quoted as saying, 'I often pray: "Lord, make me as holy as a pardoned sinner can be."' Let that be our daily prayer as the servants of God.

THINK ABOUT IT

The refusal to be committed and the attitude of indifference can in fact never be neutral.
— J. B. Phillips

I know Christ and I shall never be even; I shall die in his debt.
— Samuel Rutherford

If the doctrine of sinless perfection is a heresy, the doctrine of contentment with sinful imperfection is a greater heresy.
— *A. J. Gordon*

When all that you are is available to all that God is, then all that God is is available to all that you are.
— *Ian Thomas*

Why should we present our bodies to God's service?

On what does Paul base his appeal to us in Romans 12:1? The answer to that is very clear. It is 'by the mercies of God' that we are commanded to do so. What more moving words than these could Paul employ to set forth the duty of Christians to serve God? For eleven chapters Paul has been unfolding the mercies of almighty God. And what are they? They are precisely his acts of kindness and grace to save inexcusable and undeserving sinners like ourselves.

Let me summarize these acts of grace. Paul begins in chapters 1 to 3 by showing us that all human beings are sinful and guilty before God and deserving of his wrath and righteous judgement. For through the creation around us and our conscience within us we have all been made aware of our duty to serve God — but we deliberately suppress that knowledge in order to go our own way. And although we deserved to be condemned by God for our rebellion, he in his great mercy sent his Son Jesus Christ to do for us what we neither deserved

EXPLANATION

nor were able to do for ourselves. In an amazing act of condescension God through Jesus Christ became a man and took our sin on himself and suffered the awful God-forsaken darkness of the cross that we deserved.

But God's mercies did not stop with the giving of his Son. He also sent his Holy Spirit to deliver us from the bondage of our self-centredness and to prepare us for heaven by making us like Christ (Rom. 8). What a marvellous panorama of the mercies of God is found in Romans 1 to 11! Our salvation, Paul writes, 'does not... depend on man's desire or effort, but on God's mercy' (Rom. 9:16, NIV). And it is in view of these mercies that God in Christ has shown us, that Paul urges us to present our bodies for God's service. Our service to God does not stem from our own goodwill. It is a response to the initiative of mercy that God has already taken for our salvation. To quote a chorus I loved to sing when I was a teenager:

Out there among the hills, my Saviour died;
  Pierced by those cruel nails, was crucified.
Lord Jesus, Thou hast done all this for me,
  Henceforward I would live only for Thee.

In the New Testament, salvation is a matter of *grace* and service is a matter of *gratitude*. If we have never been overwhelmed by the sheer mercies of God we will never give ourselves unstintingly to his service. Thus Paul ends Romans 12:1 by emphasizing that the presentation of our body to God 'is our reasonable service'.

Reasonable is translated from the Greek word *logikos* from which we get our word logical. C. E. B. Cranfield says that Paul's 'point was that it was rational, as being consistent with a proper understanding of the gospel'. Concerning the word *latreian*, William Barclay says, 'this word came to be used of the service of the gods. In the Bible... it is always used of service to and worship of God.' So Paul is saying that the presentation of our body to the service of God is the only sensible, logical and appropriate response we can make in view of his self-giving mercy to us.

A life lived before the cross is a life that is constantly lived on the altar. C. T. Studd (1862–1931) was a brilliant English cricketer and Cambridge scholar who came from a very wealthy family. Yet there was a day when he signed away his vast fortune to five Christian causes and turned his back on worldly fame to preach the gospel, first in China and then in central Africa. This he did as the most reasonable thing in the world, saying, 'If Jesus Christ be God and he died for me, then there is no sacrifice which is too great for me to make for him.' This has been the response of God's people down through the history of the church. Isaac Watts speaks for us all when, in response to surveying the cross of Christ, he says in his well-loved hymn, 'Love so amazing, so divine, demands my soul, my life, my all'.

God made human beings a body-soul entity. Without a human body our soul can do absolutely nothing in this world to serve God and our fellow men. Our bodies and their members belong to Christ by a twofold right: creation and redemption. It is therefore the will of God that stewardship begins with the body and the surrender of all its parts. Christian gratitude can do no less.

———

Christianity is the total commitment of all I know of me to all I know of Jesus Christ.
— *William Temple*

QUESTIONS FOR DISCUSSION

1. *Read 1 Corinthians 3:1–16, Hebrews 5:12–14 and Luke 12:47–48 and see if you agree with this statement: It is possible to be a Christian and not be fully dedicated to God's service.*

2. *Summarize Paul's argument in Romans 6:1–23 for the necessity and importance of presenting the members of our body as 'instruments of righteousness to God'.*

3. *What light does Luke 9:57–62 throw on the decisiveness of Christian consecration?*

4. Why does Paul say that the presentation of our body should be 'a living sacrifice, holy, acceptable to God'? Make use of the following passages: Romans 6:13; 2 Timothy 2:20–26; and Ephesians 4:17–32.

5. What do we learn from 2 Corinthians 5:14–15 and Luke 7:36–50 about the main motive of Christian consecration? Give at least one other biblical example.

SUGGESTIONS FOR PRAYER

1. Thank God that as your Creator he gave you a body with which to glorify him.

2. Thank him that as your Redeemer he did not give up on you when you sold yourself as a slave of sin, but sent his dear Son to redeem you and make you one of 'his own special people, zealous for good works'.

3. Ask God to forgive you for your spasmodic and fitful service for Christ, and enable you by his Holy Spirit to live whole-heartedly to the praise of his glory until your life on earth ends.

We limit not the truth of God
   To our poor reach of mind,
By notions of our day and sect,
   Crude, partial, and confined;
No, let a new and better hope
   Within our hearts be stirred:
The Lord has yet more light and truth
   To break forth from His word.

Who dares to bind to his dull sense
   The oracles of heaven,
For all the nations, tongues, and climes,
   And all the ages given?
That universe, how much unknown!
   That ocean unexplored!
The Lord has yet more light and truth
   To break forth from His word.

O Father, Son and Spirit, send
   Us increase from above;
Enlarge, expand all Christian souls
   To comprehend Thy love:
And make us to go on to know,
   With nobler powers conferred,
The Lord has yet more light and truth
   To break forth from His word.

— George Rawson (1807–1889)

THE GUIDE

CHAPTER FOUR

THE
STEWARDSHIP
OF OUR
MIND

BIBLE REFERENCE

And do not be conformed to this world,
but be transformed by the renewing of your mind,
that you may prove what is that good
and acceptable and perfect
will of God (Rom. 12:2).

In Romans 12 the apostle Paul not only appeals to us to present our *bodies* to God for his service but he also exhorts us to 'be transformed by the renewing of your *mind*'. Why? Because we are to serve God not only through physical deeds, but also in a Christlike way that approves of God's 'good and acceptable and perfect will'. After all that is what God's stewards or servants want to do. They want to do God's will in God's way. Good deeds done in an un-Christlike way are neither pleasing to God nor a blessing to men. Character and conduct must conform to each other in the life of a steward of God.

Christlike service is the only service that is glorifying to God and of any eternal value. It is service sold out to the will of God. It is the service we are called to emulate in Philippians 2:5–8:

Let this mind be in you which was also in Christ Jesus, who, being in the form of God, did not consider it robbery to be equal with

God, but made himself of no reputation, taking the form of a bondservant, and coming in the likeness of men... he humbled himself and became obedient to the point of death, even the death of the cross.

We are to serve God like Jesus served him: with a willingness to do the will of God at any cost. Jesus approved of the will of God and abandoned himself body and soul to it.

This is what Paul is getting at in Romans 12. He is challenging us to not only surrender our bodies to God's service but also to submit our minds unreservedly to being what God wants them to be. This, however, will not happen unless our old way of thinking is changed and we begin to see that God's will is not something to shy away from but to delight in because we are convinced that it is good and acceptable and perfect.

This is another key area in our stewardship as the servants of God: the stewardship of the mind of a *person* made in God's image and not that of an *animal*. The great reformer John Calvin was a faithful steward of the mind God gave him, and this is what he had to say on the matter: 'Oh, how greatly has the man advanced who has learned not to be his own, not to be governed by his own reason, but to surrender his mind to God!'

In the past God has been pleased to use the great minds of men like Moses, David, Isaiah, Paul, Augustine, Tyndale and Luther for his glory and the good of his people. But God has equally used the minds of humble fishermen like Peter and John who were judged by the religious scholars of their day to be 'uneducated and untrained' (Acts 4:13). D. L. Moody, Billy Bray, William Nicholson and Gypsy Smith are modern examples of people who fit into this category. The human mind is a wonderful gift that God has entrusted to us for his use.

The importance of renewing our mind

EXPLANATION

It is very significant that Paul sees a vital connection between the human mind and the human body. It is a much more important connection than that which exists between the body and the brain of an animal. Paul realizes that human beings are not just creatures of instinct. Rather, the mind is the control tower that directs and governs the actions of our bodies. That is the position affirmed throughout Scripture. We read in Proverbs: 'For as he [a man] thinks in his heart, so is he' (Prov. 23:7). And the psalmist says, 'I thought about my ways, and turned my feet to your testimonies... to keep your commandments' (Ps. 119:59–60). All saving grace, the Puritans used to say, comes through the mind. 'Come now, and let us reason together, says the Lord' in Isaiah 1:18. And again: 'I will instruct you and teach you in the way you should go... Do not be like the horse or the mule, which have no understanding, which must be harnessed with bit and bridle' (Ps. 32:8–9). In Hosea 4:6 God says, 'My people are destroyed for lack of knowledge. Because you have rejected knowledge, I also will reject you from being [my] priest.' No wonder the apostle Paul, in his prayers for the Christians to whom he wrote, longs that first and foremost they might grow in knowledge. In Colossians 1:9 he says, 'We... do not cease to pray for you, and to ask that you may be filled with the knowledge of his will in all wisdom and spiritual understanding.'

God speaks to us and deals with us as rational human beings. He reasons with us, informs us, rebukes us and appeals to us. He works through our minds to get us to do his will. This is true when God saves us. How does faith come? Faith does not come through the stirring of our feelings. Paul says in Romans 10:17, 'Faith comes by hearing, and hearing by the word of God.' Sin also works on the same principle. It appeals to our mind. It convinces us that it is good, that it is all right, and that it is safe to transgress God's law.

Go back to Genesis 3 and read the story of man's fall in the Garden of Eden. How did that defeat come? How was Eve tempted? It was through her mind. The devil engaged her in conversation. By means of an argument Satan sowed doubt in her mind. He rationalized dis-obeying God's commandment. And it was when she was defeated in her thinking that very soon afterwards she was morally and spiritually defeated. This is how the evil one always operates. He blinds our minds; he insin-uates that serving God is sheer drudgery; he makes this life and all its temporary pleasures seem all important — and soon we believe him and are deceived. Indeed, as a result of the fall of Adam and Eve we are all born into this world spiritually blind. Paul writes to the Corinthians,

> If our gospel is veiled, it is veiled to those who are perishing, whose minds the god of this age has blinded, who do not believe, lest the light of the gospel of the glory of Christ, who is the image of God, should shine on them (2 Cor. 4:3–4).

In the New Testament, therefore, the new birth is essentially a giving of light and life. The Spirit of God shines into our darkened mind, and we begin to understand the truth in a way that we never understood it before. To begin with we have a *new perspective*. Before our conversion everything centred around ourselves and our personal interests. Even when we were churchgoers our thinking was self-centred. What programs does this church have to offer that are going to make me and my family happy? We did not ask: Is this a biblical church? Is God the supreme focus of the worship of this church? Am I going to become more Christlike and pleasing to God in this church? The unregenerate person is completely self-centred in his or her thinking whereas the person whose mind is renewed focuses primarily on God. God is in the centre of their thinking, and everything is tested and done according to God's will revealed in God's Word.

Another important thing is that the man or woman whose mind is being renewed has *eternity in view*. Without the renewing of our mind we could not serve God acceptably because our old unregenerate way of thinking was limited to this world. The unsaved person can only think in terms of *this world*. Everything is measured by means of material wealth and success or by physical health and happiness. The person who has been renewed by the grace of God, however, has awakened to the fact that he or she does not just belong to this world — they belong to eternity. Here we are just 'strangers and pilgrims' travelling to our home in heaven (Heb. 11:13; 1 Peter 2:11). And so we see beyond the narrow confines of this life to the life that is yet to be.

This, of course, has a radical effect on us. If we knew with absolute certainty that we only had twenty-four hours to live, it would have a dramatic effect on everything we did that day. We would prepare for eternity. But all too often death is remote from our thinking, and we tend to live as if we were going to live for ever in *this* world. The truth is that we are going to live for ever, but it will be in the *next* world, and so we ought to be living every day in this world as if it were our last. With a renewed mind we should be daily living on the threshold of eternity. We should be thinking all the time in terms of the will of God and living to do his will.

But there is another reason for the importance of the renewing of our mind. That is to give us an increasing awareness of *our utter dependence on God*. Before our conversion we were completely self-sufficient and independent. We trusted in our own wisdom and relied on our own strength and resources to do what we wanted to do. But with the renewing of our mind at our conversion we begin to see just how foolish and unable we are to understand or do the will of God. We feel the weakness of our sinful flesh, and so we pray for and rely completely on the power of the Holy Spirit to enable us to discern God's will and serve him acceptably.

THINK ABOUT IT

THINK ABOUT IT

A man is not what he thinks he is, but what he thinks, he is.
— *Anonymous*

The mind is good — God put it there. He gave us our heads and it was not his intention that our heads would function just as a place to hang a hat.
— *A. W. Tozer*

The human intellect, even in its fallen state, is an awesome work of God, but it lies in darkness until it has been illuminated by the Holy Spirit.
— *A. W. Tozer*

The means of renewing our mind

How is our mind renewed so that it can be faithfully and fruitfully used in the service of God?

How is our thinking set right? The answer the Bible gives is that our mind is being renewed in the very same way as our soul or spirit was renewed: by the operation and the *working of the Holy Spirit* (John 3:3–8; 1 John 2:20–21,26–27). But how does the Spirit renew our minds and enable us to think accurately about God, about eternity and about ourselves? How does he enable us to discern the will of God for our lives?

Initially and *negatively*, it requires the *removal* of the spiritual scales from our eyes. What a thrilling thing it is when a man or woman who is born blind in sin can see God and the things of God! Was that not the confession of the blind man in John 9 whom Jesus healed on the Sabbath? The Pharisees would not believe that Jesus had healed him because they regarded Jesus as a sinner. They said, 'This Man is not from God, because he does not keep the Sabbath.' But the healed man replied, 'Whether he is a sinner or not, I do not know. One thing I know: that though I was blind, now I see.' He was healed physically and spiritually, for his eyes were opened to see Christ as his Saviour.

Positively, however, the work of opening our eyes to the truth (to the will of God) is a *continuous* work of the Holy Spirit. It does not stop at conversion. Take the prayer of Paul for the Christians at Ephesus. He writes,

[I] do not cease to give thanks for you, making mention of you in my prayers: that the God of our Lord Jesus Christ, the Father of glory, may give to you the spirit of wisdom and revelation in the knowledge of him, the eyes of your understanding

EXPLANATION

being enlightened; that you may know what is the hope of his calling, what are the riches of the glory of his inheritance in the saints, and what is the exceeding greatness of his power toward us who believe, according to the working of his mighty power which he worked in Christ when he raised him from the dead (Ephesians 1:16–20).

There is a tremendous wealth of divine truth that the Holy Spirit must open our eyes to and correct our thinking about if we are ever to do God's will and serve him acceptably. It does not come in a flash of illumination. It is an ongoing process that lasts throughout our life on earth and will only be completed when we get to heaven and we 'shall know fully' (1 Cor. 13:12, NASB). But in the meantime, we are growing 'in the knowledge of our Lord and Saviour Jesus Christ' (2 Peter 3:18) as our minds are daily renewed by the Spirit of God.

It is important, however, to realize that the Holy Spirit does not work unaided in this process of illumination. What, then, is the aid or instrument which the Spirit of God uses to renew a Christian's mind? It is the very same instrument he used to open our eyes in the first place and bring us to faith in Christ. It is the *Word of God* (Ps. 119:105, 130,169; 2 Cor. 4:3–6). For it was through the Bible that the Holy Spirit opened our eyes to behold the beauty of Christ. Previously we saw no beauty in him that we should desire him. But when the Holy Spirit opened our spiritual eyes he showed us the loveliness of the Christ of Scripture. And the faith by which we laid hold of Jesus was a faith evoked by this Word (Rom. 10:17).

But it does not stop there. Now that we are Christians our lives are marked by a deepening grasp of the truths in God's Word as the Spirit enables us to understand them. He enables us to see how Scripture applies to our daily life so that we do not treat it just as a book of abstract truths but a book that shows us how to live in this present age according to the will of God. J. I. Packer says, 'All our minds are narrower than we think, and blind spots and obsessions abound in them like bees in clover.' So our minds need to be continually renewed and enlightened by the Spirit of God through the Word of God. This is the pathway to faithful stewardship. But because we are so reluctant and indolent as far as our study of the Bible is concerned we often fail to do and approve the will of God. God calls us to give our minds to his Word in order that the Spirit may renew our minds and enable us to go forward in the will of God. That is his means of renewing our mind.

The result of the renewing of our mind

Paul says that this renewal will bring about a marvellous spiritual transformation in our life. J. B. Phillips para-phrases it like this: 'Don't let the world around you squeeze you into its own mould, but let God remould your minds from within.' Becoming a Christian is not a religious experience that in the end leaves us unchanged. On the contrary, it involves a radical transformation of both our *character* and our *conduct*. In Romans 12:2 Paul sets before us a clear alternative. Stop being conformed to this world, and allow yourself to be continuously transformed by the renewing of your mind in accordance with God's will.

The apostle is drawing a contrast based on the fact that all human beings, by nature, are imitators. We tend to choose a model that impresses us and then we copy it. And in the end, there are only two models or criteria by which we can live. One is what Paul calls 'this world'. That is, the fleeting fashions and values of a society that has no thought for God and what he requires. It is the lifestyle of the majority that is glamourized by the media. The alternative model is what Paul calls the 'will of God' as it is revealed in the Word of God. These are the only two models that we can follow. We can either be conformed to the changing fashions of this world or be transformed by the unchanging will of God contained in his Word. There are no other alternatives. For make no mistake, the world and the Word are in fundamental conflict with one another. Between the values of the world and the will of God there is no common ground. As Christians we are to be different. We are to be

non-conformists. This is a call that is addressed to
God's people throughout Scripture. For example, in
Leviticus 18:3–4 God says to Israel,

> You shall not do... according to the doings of the
> land of Canaan, where I am bringing you... nor
> shall you walk in their ordinances. You shall observe
> my judgements and keep my ordinances, to walk in
> them: I am the Lord your God.

Another example is found in the Sermon on the Mount.
Surrounded by the false practices of both Pharisees and
pagans, Jesus said to his disciples, 'Do not be like them'
(Matt. 6:8). And now here in Romans 12 Paul issues the
same summons to God's people not to be conformed to
the way of the world but to be transformed according to
the will of God. Let me illustrate something of the
incompatibility of these two value systems. The world
says, 'Live for yourself. Get all you can.' God's Word
says, 'It is more blessed to give than to receive' (Acts
20:35). The world says that greatness is measured by
success. God's Word says that greatness is measured by
service: 'Whoever desires to become great among you,
let him be your servant' (Matt. 20:26). The world says,
'Seek after the things of this life; after food and drink
and clothes and money.' God's Word says, 'Seek first the
kingdom of God and his righteousness, and all these
things shall be added to you' (Matt. 6:23). The world
says, 'Sex is for fun. You can enjoy it without a lifelong
commitment to a spouse.' God's Word says, 'Marriage is
to be held in honor among all, and the marriage bed is

EXPLANATION

to be undefiled; for fornicators and adulterers God will judge' (Heb. 13:4, NASB).

And so I could go on. At point after point the changing fashions of the world and the unchanging will of God are so divergent that there is no possibility of compromise. We are obliged to choose. There are no other alternatives. And when we choose we are affected in one way or the other. If we choose the world we are conformed to it (we become more and more like it). If we choose God's will we are transformed more and more into the image of his Son.

The Greek word translated as transformed is *metamorphoo*, which is also the verb used by Matthew and Mark of the transfiguration of Jesus when his whole body became translucent. The only other place in Scripture where this word occurs is in 2 Corinthians 3:18. There Paul says that as we keep looking into the mirror of God's Word and see the glory of Christ (his perfect Godlikeness), we 'are being transformed into the same image from glory to glory, just as by the Spirit of the Lord'.

Do you see the logic of Paul's argument? He is saying that if you want to be transformed into Christ's image, which is the image of God, your mind must be continually renewed in understanding more and more the will of God in the life and teaching of our Lord Jesus Christ. For it is only by discerning how good and acceptable and perfect God's will is that we will gladly and willingly approve of doing it. Both verbs are present passive imperatives and denote continuing attitudes to which we are to return. We must go on refusing to conform to the world's ways and go on letting ourselves be transformed by the renewing of our mind which is made possible by the Spirit of God working through the Word of God. Only the Spirit of God opening our eyes to the will of God revealed for us in the Word of God can convince us that God's will is 'good and acceptable and perfect'.

What does that mean? It means that the Spirit of God using the Word of God will convince us that God's will is good because it has *lasting worth*. It is like comparing something that is made of solid gold with something that is merely gold-plated. The one is of sterling quality and true throughout; the other is just a shell. Likewise, what God wills for us is morally solid and of lasting worth. Now apply that to your stewardship or service. If the work you do, whether it is the work of your mind, hands or mouth, is not in accordance with God's will, it will not be solid and enduring. It will be like 'wood, hay and stubble' (1 Cor. 3:12–15) and will be burned up in the fire of the last judgement. It will not be like 'gold, silver and precious stones'. It will not be of sterling quality or have lasting worth.

Again, it is only God's Spirit through God's Word who can show us what is acceptable or *pleasing* service to God. What an acid test to apply to anyone's life! Just think of the things you have said and done recently. Can God take delight in them? It is not just a matter of doing the bare minimum of what is required of a steward of God. Does God *delight* in your service? Is it such as brings pleasure to the heart of God himself? Are you rendering him full obedience? Can you say with Jesus, 'I always do those things that please him' (John 8:29)? That is to say, you always keep God's commandments and do his will (1 John 3:22).

Then again, only the Holy Spirit through God's Word can show us what is perfect service. That is to say, service that is in *complete conformity* to God's will. It is consistent with his character. It does not bring shame or disgrace on the name of God. It is service that expresses completely and perfectly the will of our heavenly Father who is perfect.

One final thing to notice is that this is a *command* not a request. This is God's will for Christian stewardship. To be good and acceptable and perfect to God, it must involve not only the surrender of our bodies to him but our minds as well. This should be our great desire: that we might so give ourselves to God for the renewing of our minds that we will come to know and approve God's good and acceptable and perfect will. And in doing it be increasingly transformed by it into the image of Christ, the perfect Servant of the Lord. Faithful Christian stewardship not only benefits God and those we serve, it also benefits us. We are the better for serving God according to his will. No one is ever the poorer for doing so, only the richer (if it is true and lasting riches you are concerned about).

The practical effect of a renewed mind on our service

Mindlessness is a menace to Christian life and service. It impoverishes our worship, weakens our faith and renders our witness ineffective. Consider first, *our worship of God*. Jesus said to the Samaritan woman at Jacob's well, 'You worship what you do not know... God is Spirit, and those who worship him must worship in spirit and truth' (John 4:22,24). True Christian worship, whether public or private, must be spiritual and rational. It must engage the heart through the mind. That is why the Reformers in the sixteenth century brought the Word of God back to the worship of God. They knew that it is the Word of God (the truth) that evokes the worship of God. To grow in our knowledge of God should not puff us up with conceit at how knowledgeable we are but rather result in our prostration before God in sheer wonder and crying, 'Great is the Lord, and greatly to be praised; and his greatness is unsearchable' (Ps. 145:3).

The apostle Paul also insisted on the engagement of the mind in our worship of God. He forbade speaking in tongues in public worship if there was no one to translate or interpret the prayer that had been prayed in an unknown language. He even discourages its exercise in private if the speaker himself is unable to interpret what he is praying. In 1 Corinthians he says,

> Unless you utter by the tongue words easy to understand, how will it be known what is spoken? ... Therefore let him who speaks in a tongue pray that he may interpret. For if I pray in a tongue, my spirit prays, but my understanding [mind] is unfruitful. What is the conclusion then? I will pray with the spirit, and I will also pray with the understanding [mind] (1 Cor. 14:9,13–15)

EXPLANATION

In other words, Paul would not sanction any prayer in which the mind is barren or inactive. He insists that in all true worship the mind must be fully engaged for it is the worship of a rational God who has made us rational beings and given us a rational revelation in order that we may worship him rationally. For this reason, therefore, the only perfect worship that is offered to God is in heaven, not on earth, because it is only in heaven that God is clearly seen and fully known.

Again, a proper use of the mind *strengthens our faith*. Faith is not blind credulity. Many people put faith and reason in opposition to one another. But this is wrong because in the New Testament faith and *sight* are contrasted. Faith and a proper use of the mind are never contrasted. In Scripture, true faith is essentially reasonable because it rests on the character and promises of God. And since God is trustworthy, trust in God must be reasonable.

Nor is faith naive optimism. The equation of faith and optimism is, I fear, the mistake made by Norman Vincent Peale. By and large much of what Dr. Peale says is true and helpful. The power of positive thinking is a very real fact of life. But Dr. Peale does not seem to draw any distinction between faith in God and faith in yourself. The first chapter of his book *The Power of Positive Thinking* is significantly entitled, 'Believe in yourself'. He recommends that first thing every morning you should get up and say to yourself, 'I believe', but he does not tell us *what* or in *whom* we are to believe. To Dr. Peale faith is another word for self-confidence, and his definition of positive thnking is in reality merely wishful thinking. The apostle Paul, on the other hand, says, 'Faith comes by hearing, and hearing by the word of God' (Rom. 10:17). That is to say, faith comes by thinking on what God says and coming to the conclusion that it is the truth and can be relied on. Little wonder that Adlai Stevenson, the former American ambassador to the United Nations, once quipped, 'I find Paul appealing, but Peale appalling!'

Faith is a reasonable trust in the God who has been fully and finally revealed in Jesus Christ. In the Bible faith and thought belong together — believing in God does not require us to be gullible and uncritical. Jesus is quite clear about this in Matthew 6:30 when he says, 'Now if God so clothes the grass of the field, which today is, and tomorrow is thrown into the oven, will he not much more clothe you, O you of little faith.' The trouble with those who have little faith is precisely that they do not think properly. Instead of their mind being controlled by the revelation of God in Scripture and in nature, their mind is being controlled by their circumstances or by Satan's fiery darts of doubt. The essence of unbelief is not thought but the failure to think biblically and realistically.

Yet again, a proper use of our mind is *essential for effective witness*. Much Christian evangelism over the years has failed in the long run because it has been an assault on people's emotions rather than an appeal to their minds. The apostles were careful to avoid this mistake. Their sermons (recorded in Acts) are wonderful examples of well thought out arguments urging their hearers to repent of their sin and to believe in Christ as God's long-promised Saviour. In 2 Corinthians 5:11 Paul sums up his own preaching ministry as 'knowing... the terror of the Lord, we persuade men'. To persuade is to gather facts together with a view to convincing people to believe something and act on it. It is an intellectual exercise. Indeed, all the words that Luke uses in Acts to describe Paul's witness to Christ bear this out. He writes of Paul arguing, proving, disputing, reasoning and persuading. Moreover, the New Testament often speaks of conversion not only in terms of a person's commitment to Christ but of their 'believing the truth', or 'obeying the truth' or 'acknowledging the truth'.

So it is through the truth we preach and the arguments we deploy that the Holy Spirit convicts men and women and convinces them to come to

Christ in faith. An otherwise unconvincing message cannot have the power to persuade anyone to believe on the name of Christ simply by appealing to the Holy Spirit to do so. The persuasiveness of our message can only come from its contents. Where this is not the case, an appeal to the Holy Spirit will not avail. Dr Martyn Lloyd-Jones put it well when he said,

> No subject is discussed more often than power in preaching. 'Oh, that I might have power in preaching', says the preacher, and he goes on his knees and prays for power. I think that this may be quite wrong! It certainly is if it is the only thing that the preacher does. The way to have power is to prepare your message carefully. Study the Word of God, think it out, analyze it, put it in order, do your utmost. That is the message God is most likely to bless.

Let us be wise stewards of the minds God has so graciously given to us. To neglect this gift is to condemn ourselves to spiritual poverty and to rob God as well as others of much blessing from our service. What we need is not less knowledge but more knowledge, provided we use it to enrich our worship, strengthen our faith and make our witness to Christ more effective.

KEY THOUGHTS

Any Christian service rendered in an un-Christlike way is neither acceptable to God nor a blessing to men. But to become more and more like Christ our minds need to be continually renewed by the Spirit of God who uses the Word of God to convince our minds to submit to the will of God as revealed therein. As we do so we prove that God's will is 'good and acceptable and perfect' and both we and our service are considerably enriched. On the other hand, mindless Christianity is the greatest menace to God-pleasing and God-honouring service for it cannot know or do the will of God.

QUESTIONS FOR DISCUSSION

DISCUSS IT

1. What is the spiritual condition of our mind from birth to our conversion or regeneration? See Ephesians 4:17–24; Romans 1:20–23.

2. How does an unregenerate mind view the will of God? See Romans 8:5–8.

3. Give some examples of how a renewed mind influences our lives.

4. Give at least two Scripture references for each of the following:
    a. Who does the work of renewing a Christian's mind?
    b. What is the main instrument involved in the process?
    c. Is it a one-time experience?
    d. What is the ultimate result of the renewing of our mind?

SUGGESTIONS FOR PRAYER

1. *Praise God for giving you a mind that, through his Spirit and Holy Scripture, can know who he is and why he created you.*

2. *Thank him that by the grace of Christ he has illuminated your spiritually darkened mind and revealed himself and his will to you.*

3. *Ask him to forgive your carelessness in resisting the pressure to conform to the world and seeking to be conformed more and more to Christ.*

4. *Pray for strength to commit yourself to the good and acceptable and perfect will of God and become a better steward of the mind that he has entrusted to you for his glory.*

Must I go, and empty-handed,
Thus my dear Redeemer meet,
Not one day of service give Him,
Lay no trophy at His feet?

Not at death I shrink nor falter,
For my Saviour saves me now;
But to meet Him empty-handed,
Thought of that now clouds my brow.

O the years in sinning wasted,
Could I but recall them now,
I would give them to my Saviour,
To His will I'd gladly bow.

O ye saints, arouse, be earnest,
Up and work while yet 'tis day;
Ere the night of death o'ertake thee,
Strive for souls while still you may.

> *Must I go, and empty-handed?*
> *Must I meet my Saviour so?*
> *Not one soul with which to greet Him:*
> *Must I empty-handed go?*

— *Charles C. Luther (1847–1924)*

THE GUIDE

CHAPTER FIVE

THE STEWARDSHIP OF OUR TALENTS

LOOK IT UP

BIBLE REFERENCE

For I say, through the grace given to me,
to everyone who is among you, not to think of himself
more highly than he ought to think, but to think
soberly, as God has dealt to each one a measure of
faith. For as we have many members in one body,
but all the members do not have the same function,
so we, being many, are one body in Christ,
and individually members of one another.
Having then gifts differing according to the grace
that is given to us, let us use them
(Rom. 12:3–6).

INTRODUCTION

It is very significant that in Romans 12 the apostle
Paul moves from the presenting of our bodies to
the renewing of our minds to the using of our gifts
or talents. For the renewing of our mind is not
only necessary for discerning and approving
God's will for our lives but also for soberly
evaluating our gifts.

A renewed mind is both humble and honest.
It enables us to have a true understanding of our
place in the church, which is the body of Christ,
and the abilities God has given to us to fulfil that
function or service. In verse 3 the Greek verb
phronein (to think) is repeated three times to
emphasize the fact that to think with a sober mind
about ourselves we must avoid both too high an
estimate of ourselves and (Paul might have added)

too low an estimate. That is what we want to consider: a proper understanding of the stewardship of our talents or abilities in the service of Christ and his church.

Have you ever thought about the fact that the church of Jesus Christ is the only society in the world in which no inactive members are allowed? Every member is active and vital to the functioning of the church. That is the clear teaching of many of our Lord's parables, especially those of the talents and the pounds or minas. Unfortunately many church members picture the local church as a pyramid, with the pastor at the apex and the deacons and the rest of the congregation in their serried ranks of inferiority beneath him. Other members picture their church as a bus with the pastor driving and the church family enjoying the ride. But the bus and the pyramid models are not biblical models of the church.

The church is the household of faith in which every member is a servant and steward charged with a partic-ular function to perform and given the resources with which to complete the task. Paul's favourite model of the church, when he is thinking about the spiritual gifts that God has given to every Christian, is to see it as the *body* of Christ. It is a body that has Christ as its head and every Christian as a member (an organ or limb) of that body with a function to fulfil (Rom. 12:4–8; 1 Cor. 12:12–31; Eph. 4:4–16).

Some churches indicate their staff in their bulletin in this unique way: 'Pastor, John Smith; Ministers, the entire congregation'. That is biblical. Every member of Christ's church is an active minister or servant of his. Paul says, 'For as we have many members in one body, but all the members do not have the same function, so we, being many, are one body in Christ, and individually members of one another' (Rom. 12:4–5). That is, every member is dependent on every other member for the health and enrichment of the whole. Just as every member of the human body has a specific function to perform, so every member of the body of Christ has an important role to play in order for that body to function in the way God intends it to. No Christian should fall into the devil's trap of thinking that they have no useful gift to employ in the service of edifying the body of Christ and enabling it to fulfil its God-given function of evangelizing the world.

Some of us may feel we have no gifts of any consequence. We may say, 'If I could preach I would be a pastor. If I were any good at languages I would be a missionary. If I were musical I would join the choir or be an accompanist. If I were an academic I would be a theologian. If I were not so shy I would witness to others. But God has given me so little it is not worth trying.'

The story is told of two cockney boys who were protesting their lifelong devotion to each other. The first little boy said to the other, 'Hey, Bobby, if you 'ad a million pounds, would you give me 'alf?' 'Course I would', Bobby replied. 'What about if you 'ad a fousand pounds?' 'I'd give you 'alf just the same.' 'What about if you 'ad a fousand marbles?' 'I'd give 'alf of 'em also.' 'What about if you 'ad two marbles?' 'That's

not fair', complained Bobby. 'You know I've only got
two marbles!'

God wants our two marbles. He is not interested in
the hypothetical devotion that we would exercise if
only we had a lot of material resources and spiritual
gifts at our disposal. He wants the talents we have to be
dedicated to his service. Only in this way will we have
anything to show on the last day as evidence that we
were trustworthy and good servants. That is clearly the
warning in the parables of the talents and the minas
(Matt. 25:14–30; Luke 19:11–27). Both servants who
failed to use the resources their master gave them were
severely reprimanded and their talent or mina taken
away and given to those servants who had served their
master more faithfully.

This sounds unfair. Why should their talent or mina
be given to someone who already has plenty? Jesus,
however, is simply illustrating a spiritual principle that
he repeats many times: 'For to everyone who has, more
will be given, and he will have abundance; but from
him who does not have, even what he has will be taken
away' (Matt. 25:29). In other words, you cannot please
God if you do nothing with your life and talents. The
only people who are going to be rewarded in eternity
are those who are willing to use what God has given
them to serve his ends and not theirs. Any Christian
who is not involved in the work of Christ's church and
is only a pew warmer or a sermon taster is at best going
to be saved 'as through fire' (1 Cor. 3:15).

Luke's account of the story actually leaves the final
destiny of this servant in some doubt, but in Matthew's

version of the parable there is a far less optimistic end. Jesus says, 'Cast the unprofitable servant into the outer darkness. There will be weeping and gnashing of teeth' (Matt. 25:30). A person who professes to be a Christian but does nothing at all to advance the cause of Christ is probably not a Christian at all. The irony of the faithless servant who did not want to take the risk of losing his master's talent (or not using it profitably), is that he took the biggest risk of all: gambling with his soul. Dr Martyn Lloyd-Jones says, 'The man who tries to do something and fails is infinitely better than the man who tries to do nothing and succeeds.'

As we turn to the proper stewardship of our abilities, let us begin with the source of our talents.

The source of our talents

The apostle Peter says, 'As each one has received a gift, minister it to one another, as good stewards of the manifold grace of God' (1 Peter 4:10). We have no ability or skill that is of our own making or deserving. God has freely given us everything we have and are. There is no room for boasting about our talents. This is Paul's teaching as well: 'For who makes you differ from another? And what do you have that you did not receive? Now if you did indeed receive it, why do you boast as if you had not received it?' (1 Cor. 4:7).

Now if all our abilities come from God, how do we receive them? There are at least three channels of supply. The first, of course, is *by birth*. We are all born physically with some talent. You are either musical or you are not. You are either mechanically minded or you are not. You are either an organizer or you are not. You are either artistic or you are not, and so we could go on. Moreover, there is not too much we can do about these naturally inherited abilities. We can improve what has been given to us, but we cannot create what is not there.

That, however, is not our only source of talents. For in the second place we can *acquire* certain talents. No one is born with a natural talent for typing, nursing, printing, writing, building, and so on. These are skills you can learn with training and practice. But they are all abilities that can be used for God. A church secretary can save a pastor valuable time for prayer and Bible study by using skills like shorthand and typing. Nursing, printing and building are abilities sorely needed on the mission field.

Then again, in the third place, we can receive abilities *through God's Spirit*. Himself *the* gift of God, one of his chief functions is to give gifts to God's children. There are at least twenty-one different gifts of the Spirit mentioned in five separate lists in the New Testament. These are the word of wisdom, the word of knowledge, faith, healing, miracles, prophecy, distinguishing of spirits, tongues, interpretation of tongues (1 Cor. 12:8–10), apostles, prophets, teachers, helps, administrations (1 Cor. 12:28), serving, exhortation, giving, leading, mercy (Rom. 12:1–8), evangelists and pastors (Eph. 4:11). The fifth list is in 1 Peter 4:10–11, but no new gifts are mentioned.

EXPLANATION

Moreover, because celibacy is mentioned as a separate gift in 1 Corinthians 7:7 and each list has some gifts that are not mentioned in the other, there is good reason to believe that we do not have an exhaustive list of gifts in the New Testament. Dr Martyn Lloyd-Jones points out that prayer is not listed, and surely the gift to write Christian books and the gift to compose the lyrics and music for spiritual songs should also be classified as gifts of the Spirit. It is a great mistake then to be preoccupied with only three gifts (namely, tongues, healing and prophecy) as some people are. It is also a mistake to say that there are only nine gifts of the Spirit — those found in 1 Corinthians 12:8–10. We have no liberty to ignore the other lists of Spirit gifts found elsewhere in the New Testament. Indeed, the rule that Paul gives us in 1 Corinthians 14 is that all gifts are to be evaluated according to their ability to edify the entire body of believers. The more a gift edifies the church the greater it is (1 Cor. 14:5). One further clarification: revelatory gifts like apostles and prophets ceased to be given once all the books of the Bible were completed.

So in addition to natural gifts (abilities we are born with) and acquired gifts (abilities we can learn), God also imparts to us spiritual gifts (abilities only the Spirit can give). In fact, the New Testament reveals that each Christian has at least one spiritual gift. 'As each one has received a special gift, employ it in serving one another'

(1 Peter 4:10, NASB). Or again, 'All these [gifts] are inspired by one and the same Spirit, who apportions to each one individually as he wills' (1 Cor. 12:11, RSV). Or yet again, 'For I say... to everyone who is among you... having then gifts differing according to the grace that is given to us, let us use them' (Rom. 12:3,6). All of us, therefore, have at least one spiritual gift even if we have not yet discovered it. Moreover, it does not have to remain at just one gift. Although we each have a gift, Paul exhorts us twice to earnestly desire spiritual gifts (1 Cor. 12:31; 14:39).

The implication of these truths is that a Christian who opts out of all service in the church and tries to hide behind the excuse that he or she has nothing to offer is guilty of calling God a liar. They are denying the obvious truth that every Christian has not only natural abilities and acquired skills but also spiritual gifts. And he or she is a victim of false humility. For as Spiros Zodhiates in *The Song of the Virgin* says,

> If you're leading a useless life, you're not being humble. You're just plain lazy... Many a man, while seriously believing that he was exercising an acceptable humility, has buried his talents in the earth and lived a useless life, when he might have been a blessing to many. Our humility serves us falsely when it leads us to shrink from any duty. The plea of unfitness or inability is utterly insufficient to excuse us... Your talent may be very small. So small that it scarcely seems to matter whether you use it or not, so far as its impression on other

lives is concerned. Yet no one can know what is small and what is great in this life, in which every cause starts consequences that reach into eternity.

Those are true and searching words. Do they convict you of your lack of commitment to Christ and your self-preoccupation when the world is going to hell and the church is desperately short of workers?

The purpose of our talents

Many people behave as if they have received their talents to benefit themselves, as if the gifts that they have are purely for their own enjoyment and advancement. That is not the perspective that the Bible declares. Peter says, 'As each one has received a special gift, employ it in serving one another' (1 Peter 4:10, NASB). Our motto is, 'From each according to his or her ability'. Our talents were not given to us so that we could accumulate a lot of money or make a great name for ourselves. Our talents were given to us for the good of Christ's church. 'The manifestation of the Spirit is given to each one for the profit of all [or for the common good]' (1 Cor. 12:7). John Calvin says, 'Whatever ability a faithful Christian may possess, he ought to possess it for his fellow believers, and he ought to make his own

EXPLANATION

interest subservient to the well-being of the church in all sincerity.'

But there is an even higher reason. Our talents were given to us to glorify God, and the greatest way we can bring glory to God is to use our gifts or talents for the good of all. Jane Stuart Smith is an American soprano from Virginia whose operatic career took her to all the major opera houses in America and Europe. She was a world-acclaimed star. One day, however, on her way to the Milan Opera House, the plane in which she was flying developed engine trouble and was forced to crash-land. During those frightening moments she made a pact with God that if he got her out of that situation alive, she would give her life to him.

In the goodness of God she survived that crash-landing and followed through on her vow to God by joining a Bible study group in Milan. Later she came to hear of L'Abri Fellowship in Huemoz, Switzerland, and spent a weekend there. 'She became a Christian here', Francis Schaeffer wrote in the foreword of a book she co-authored, 'and was instrumental in opening the first door for us to work among the musicians in Milan, and then eventually to the beginning of a Bible study class there. Later she became a worker in L'Abri and then later still a member of L'Abri... There are people all over the world who now understand something of classical music and have a deep enjoyment of it because of their times at Chalet Chesalet. Jane Stuart Smith has added a very special musical contribution to L'Abri.'

That is why God has given us talents (natural, acquired and spiritual), not to glorify ourselves but to glorify God by using them for the common good of the church and even those outside the church.

THINK ABOUT IT

If we listen to the instruction of Scripture, we must remember that our talents are not of our own making, but free gifts of God.
— *John Calvin*

We are all talented people. Anything whereby we may glorify God is a talent.
— *J. C. Ryle*

Spiritual gifts are not toys with which to play; they are tools of the Spirit with which to do the Lord's work effectively.
— *G. Raymond Carlson*

Discovering our talents

There are many ways to discover your talents, but let me suggest three. The first is through *prayerful thought*. Get alone, take a piece of paper and put a line down the middle. At the top of the left half put the heading, 'What I can do', and at the top of the right half put the heading, 'What I can't do'. Then start writing and see how much you can put in each column. Do it prayerfully and honestly, allowing the Holy Spirit to check what you write down. For some things that you think you cannot do, he may well show you that with God's help you can. Some of the things that you think you can do, he may help you to see that you cannot.

Second, *seek an outside opinion* on this list from those who know you and love you. They must know you well to be in a position to advise you as to what your gifts truly are. And they must love you to be able to tell you what you cannot do in a way that will not discourage you.

In the third place, *get involved*. Accept the job that you feel God is calling you to do, and by faith seek to do it. You will never learn whether you are able to do a particular service for God if you do not try. It is the only way that you can learn not only how to do the job but also whether you have the ability or not. That is how I began to teach and preach. I was asked to give a five-minute message in the church's open-air meeting at the Johannesburg railway station in South Africa. The first Sunday I had to speak, my mind went completely blank. I forgot all I had planned to say, and after an embarrassing silence that seemed to last an eternity, I just said, 'God loves you and wants to save you!' Wisely, our leader came to me afterwards and said, 'Brian, I want you to speak next week, otherwise you'll never get the courage to do it again.'

That is how I got started. I made mistakes, but by faith I gave it a try. And it is the only way that you too will find out whether you have a gift or not. It is by involvement. It is by going out in faith and trying to serve the

EXPLANATION

Lord — take a Sunday school class when the teacher is absent, for example. That is how you find out if you have the gift of preaching, teaching, ruling, praying in public, or whatever it may be. It is not by some dream or special revelation from God. It is by starting in some small way to do what God's Spirit is leading you to do.

I must emphasize that there are some jobs — such as preaching in the church — that require a special calling from God. The divine call will come first, as you become spiritually aware through your daily devotions that God is moving you by his Spirit to preach his Word. Then you must check the reality of that conviction against the requirements God has laid down in Scripture for preachers. For example, you must be a man and you must be truly converted to Christ. Added to this is the fact that if it is a calling from God, it will only increase until you respond to it and trust God to bring out of you the spiritual gift he has given you.

Knowing where to exercise our talents

We should not begin using our talents where they will be most noticed or appreciated. It is a very subtle temptation to be in the public view and to be applauded. But that is not what guides a Christian. A Christian is guided by the will of God as revealed in his Word. The will of God is that our talents should be used first in the home. Paul says in 1 Timothy 5:8, 'But if anyone does not provide for his own, and especially for those of his household, he has denied the faith and is worse than an unbeliever.' The apostle, of course, does not merely have in mind a mother or father's ability to provide food, clothing and shelter for their family but also spiritual instruction and guidance.

It may seem like a small stage, but our first responsibility is to our family. I dishonour God and misuse my gifts if I am so eager to preach to the crowds that I have no time to teach my own children. Our children have first claim on our time and talents. As we fulfil our responsibilities as parents, only eternity will reveal how far-reaching the effects will be. Susannah Wesley, the mother of John and Charles Wesley, was an amazing woman who gave two hours per week to teach each of her nineteen children (of whom nine died in infancy). In the kitchen of the vicarage of Epworth she also had services in which she would read to them a chapter from the Bible as well as a sermon from a book. So if you want to know the secret of John and Charles Wesley's great usefulness in the kingdom, it is partly because of a mother who used her talents in the home.

Next, it is God's will that our talents should be used in our spiritual home or church family. Every epistle in the New Testament enjoins Christians to use their gifts in their local church. To fail to do so is as bad as not taking care of your own family. For God has put us in a church family to provide for all its needs (spiritual, emotional, practical and financial). If we fail to make our contribution, our spiritual home is going to suffer. It will be handicapped by the withholding of our services and will function like a body that has lost a limb or two. But did not God create that body? And did he not give it members to serve the body without thought to themselves? Of course he did. How, then, can we refuse to serve the body in which God has placed us?

Maximizing our talents

EXPLANATION

The obvious way to make the most of our talents is to use them. Paul writes, 'Having then gifts differing according to the grace that is given to us, let us use them' (Rom. 12:6). Any talent will atrophy if it is not used. Second, use them as long as possible. Here I want to express a word of caution born of experience. There are many times when we can stop using our gifts, but two of the most frequent are when we move house or when we retire. What happens is that we can be so busy in work at our church that when we move house and transfer to another church we immediately say, 'Now, here's a chance to get a little break from serving in the church.' But this is very wrong. When we move house, God wants us to move our talents to the new church for that is our new spiritual home; this is the new body of believers we are to serve. It is wrong, too, because more often than not our lack of involvement lasts longer than we intended. It is easy to become accustomed to sitting back and taking it easy.

It is the same with retirement. Although retirement is a time to ease up on our secular responsibilities, it is not a time to ease up on the Lord's work. Rather it can often free our schedules to enable us to do more work for the Lord than was previously possible. Of course, I am not suggesting that you should hang on to your job in the church forever. No, that is not good either — a change of office is sometimes needed. But if you want a change, volunteer to do some other job in the church where your abilities lie. None of us needs a year's rest or more from serving the Lord. Time is short and the work is urgent; therefore we must not spare ourselves.

The subject of this chapter is a most important one. Having pastored six churches, it is my sad experience that too many people want to do as little as possible in their church. They are taken up with abounding in their own work when according to Paul they ought to be 'always abounding in the work of the Lord' (1 Cor. 15:58). That is, doing as much Christian work as the Lord gives us and that we can make time for. 'Work... while it is day', Jesus said, '[for] the night is coming when no one can work' (John 9:4).

Surely this is an appropriate word for Christians today. It is so difficult to get twenty-first century Christians to do the many jobs that need to be done for the Lord and his church today. We are all so busy that we just do not seem to be able to find time for serving God. If we had our priorities right we would be busy doing the Lord's work — not accumulating and pursuing the things that this world values. After all, we are not our own masters. We are God's servants. And nothing is so reprehensible as a servant who uses his Master's time and tools to serve himself.

What a fearful prospect the day of reckoning will be for such a servant! Without a doubt, when that day comes we will have to 'give an account of [our] stewardship' (Luke 16:2). Paul backs this up in 2 Corinthians 5:10 when he says, 'For we must all appear before the judgement seat of Christ, that each one may receive the things done in the body... whether good or bad.' The judgement Paul speaks of here does not envisage the loss of a Christian's soul. It is the judgement of a Christian's works: 'what he has done' (NIV). This is made very clear in 1 Corinthians 3:15.

No true steward will fail to enter into heaven. But there will be a difference in the rewards that each one will receive. For the works, says Paul, are going to be tested by fire. If a man's works are precious because they bring glory to God and build up the church, they will come through the fire (like silver or gold) and he will receive a reward. But if a man's works are worthless because they did not glorify God, they will be burned up (like wood, hay and stubble). 'He will suffer loss', says Paul, 'but he himself will be saved, yet so as through fire.'

But please note that God will reward us according to our *faithfulness* — not according to our *successfulness*. For, says Paul, it is required of stewards that they be found faithful (1 Cor. 4:2). The Lord will reward his servants not according to the *greatness* of their gift but according to the *time and effort* that they have put into his work. Let us therefore live and work for the day when we will hear our Master say, 'Well done, good and faithful servant... enter into the joy of your Lord' (Matt. 25:23).

A certain medical student achieved his university degree with distinction. All his friends predicted a very bright future: further degrees and a high paying job. But to their great surprise he announced that he was going to the mission field. Amazed that he should turn his back on such great prospects they said, 'But that's no way to get on in the world.' His reply was simple and unanswerable, 'Which world?'

THINK ABOUT IT

Only one life, 'twill soon be past;
Only what's done for Christ will last.
— *C. T. Studd*

QUESTIONS FOR DISCUSSION

1. *What is the connection between the renewing of my mind and the proper use of my talents? See Romans 12:1–8.*

EXPLANATION

2. *If God is the source of all our gifts, in what way do we acquire them? Give scriptural examples and references to back up your answers.*

3. *Read Romans 12:4–8, 1 Corinthians 12:12–31 and Ephesians 4:4–16. What lessons about our God-given gifts does Paul draw from the metaphor that the church is Christ's body?*

4. *A failure to use our gifts to glorify God can have serious eternal consequences. Use Matthew 25:14–30 and 1 Corinthians 3:9–15 to describe in your own words what those consequences could be.*

SUGGESTIONS FOR PRAYER

1. *Thank God the Father for the gifts he has entrusted to you and ask for his forgiveness in not using them as well as you could have to honour him and build up Christ's church.*

2. *Pray for grace to make yourself available to the leaders of your local church and for guidance as to where your abilities can be best put to use.*

Only one life to offer — Jesus, my Lord and King;
Only one tongue to praise Thee and of Thy mercy sing;
Only one heart's devotion — Saviour, O may it be
Consecrated alone to Thy matchless glory,
 Yielded fully to Thee.

Only this hour is mine, Lord — may it be used for Thee;
May every passing moment count for eternity;
Souls all about are dying, dying in sin and shame;
Help me bring them the message of Calvary's redemption
 In Thy glorious name.

Only one life to offer — take it, dear Lord, I pray;
Nothing from Thee withholding, Thy will I now obey.
Thou who hast freely given Thine all in all for me,
Claim this life for Thine own to be used, my Saviour,
 Every moment for Thee.

— *Avis B. Christiansen (1895–1985)*

CHAPTER SIX

THE
STEWARDSHIP
OF OUR
TIME

BIBLE REFERENCE

To everything there is a season,
A time for every purpose under heaven
(Eccles. 3:1).

See then that you walk circumspectly [or carefully],
not as fools but as wise, redeeming the time,
because the days are evil.
Therefore do not be unwise,
but understand what the will of the Lord is
(Eph. 5:15–17).

Time began with the creation of the world. As such, it is a precious gift entrusted to us by our Creator for his glory. It is a fragment of eternity given by God to humankind as a solemn stewardship, and one day God will call each one of us to give an account of how we have used it. The difference between one steward and another will depend largely on their use of time. All achievements for God are conditioned upon a wise use of time. If we fail here we fail everywhere. No person can do more than their time on earth allows them. In his *Holy Living*, Jeremy Taylor wrote, 'God hath given to man a short time here upon earth and yet upon this short time eternity depends. No man is a better merchant than he that lays out his time upon God.'

The importance of time

Time cannot be stretched. Time is a fixed commodity. For every single one of us each hour has 60 minutes, each day has 24 hours and each year has 365 days. It is the same for everybody. No matter how much we may wish we could be like Joshua and make the sun stand still, we cannot. None of us can fit more time into a single day. We may feel that life is too short for us to do everything that we want to do, but it is long enough for us to do everything God wants us to do.

Another sobering thing about time is that it can be lost, and lost time can never be regained. Time passes, but once it is past, it is lost, irretrievably lost. Some years ago a spurious advertisement appeared in an American journal in the 'Lost and Found' column. It read: 'Lost yesterday, somewhere between sunrise and sunset, two golden hours, each set with sixty diamond minutes. No reward offered, for they are gone forever.'

Wise Christians realize this. They know that their time is passing. In Ephesians 5:16 wise Christians are described as those who are 'making the most of time' (NASB). Thomas Edison, the Christian whose workshop changed the world, said, 'Time is not a commodity that can be stored for future use. It must be invested hour by hour or else it is gone for ever.' Or, to quote Stephen Charnock, 'What is past cannot be recalled; what is future cannot be insured.' Each day God opens a new account in the bank named Time. He allows no balances and no overdrafts. If we fail to use the day's deposit the loss is ours.

But even more importantly, we must see time as *belonging to God*. We will never get anywhere in our Christian life if we think that only a portion of our time belongs to God and that if we give God his portion (Sunday), the rest of the week is ours. That is not biblical Christianity. In the words of George Herbert's old hymn, true Christianity is, 'Seven whole days, not one in seven, I will praise Thee.'

Paul saw himself and every Christian as a slave of Jesus Christ — one who has been 'bought at a price' (1 Cor. 7:23). To be bought means that Christ has claim to all of our time. But having said that, it is Christ's will for us to use our time for different purposes.

I think the key consideration in the use of our time is *balance*. But properly balancing all of our God-given responsibilities is a very difficult thing to achieve. In some ways it is easier to give all your time to one thing rather than dividing your time properly between all of life's responsibilities. How, then, are we to wisely use our time?

Essential personal demands on our time

Although there are higher priorities, God expects us to spend time on ourselves. The things that come to mind are the following essentials.

1. Sleeping

Most of us spend a third of our life in bed. And often we
are tempted to think that it is a waste of time. But of
course it is not. We may try to burn the midnight oil,
but we cannot go for too long without proper sleep. Our
bodies and our minds need rest, and they only function
properly when they receive the right amount of rest.

The amount of time needed for sleep will vary with
each individual, but whatever amount is needed, God
expects us to take it. True, it is not his purpose that we
overindulge in sleep, just as it is not his purpose that
we overindulge in anything (whether food, drink, sex
or worldly possessions). The sluggard is roundly
condemned in the book of Proverbs, particularly in
chapter 6:6–11. When he is woken up in the morning
and asked, 'How long will you slumber, O sluggard?
When will you rise up from your sleep?' He replies, 'A
little sleep, a little slumber, a little folding of the hands
to sleep.' He does not refuse to get up. He does not even
ask to spend the morning in bed. All he asks for is just
another minute or two to fold his hands and sleep. In
his commentary on Proverbs, Derek Kidner writes: 'He
deceives himself by the smallness of his surrenders.' He
is not asking for much, just a little more sleep. What
he forgets, the book of Proverbs says, is that if he
overindulges in sleep, 'poverty will come upon him, like
a bandit and scarcity like an armed man' (NIV).

To give the proper amount of time that we need for
sleep is never a waste of time according to the Bible,
for God created the night for us to rest. Moreover, not
only are both body and mind refreshed, but often

EXPLANATION

during our sleep God provides the solutions to our problems. All of us, I am sure, have known times when we went to bed with a problem and woke up with the solution. And it is in testimony to this that Psalm 127:2 says, 'It is vain for you to rise up early, to retire late... for he [God] gives to his beloved even in his sleep' (NASB). But more to the point, the rest of sleep is the reward of fruitful labour. Or as Robert Murray M'Cheyne put it: 'Oh, how sweet to work all day for God, and then lie down at night beneath his smile!'

2. Eating

Have you ever worked out how many hours you spend on meals? It is quite a large proportion. But it, too, is time well spent. People who rush their meals will soon have ulcers. People who do not prepare their meals properly and do not eat a balanced diet will suffer to some extent from various physical disorders. It is as simple as that. To quote Adele Davis, a well-known American dietitian, 'Many people are digging their own graves with a knife and fork.'

I can personally but sadly vouch for this. For twelve years in the early part of my pastoral ministry, I was diagnosed with indogenous depression by doctors and psychiatrists in three different cities. I was mentally tired in the day but could not sleep at night. My medications ranged from Librium to lithium, but nothing helped. I remained as mentally fatigued as ever. Eventually I had to resign from my pastorate. During an eleven month leave of absence my wife got the idea from a magazine article that my problem was excessive caffeine (a two-litre bottle of regular Coca-Cola a day) and not enough calcium from dairy products. Since rectifying this I have had no further trouble with sleeping at night or being too tired to think during the day. A simple correction of my diet has enabled me to give my best efforts to the last twenty-five years of ministry in the pastorate.

Time and thought for proper eating is not a luxury but a necessity. Both the length and the usefulness of our lives depend on it. In Mark 6:31 Jesus said to his disciples, '"Come aside by yourselves to a deserted place and rest awhile." For there were many coming and going and they did not even have time to eat.'

3. Working
Everybody is a worker. Nobody can live without working. Next to sleep, the largest percentage of our time is spent working. This, too, for the Christian is not wasted time. We need to work to keep ourselves alive. Although God gives us our daily bread, it does not fall from heaven into our laps — we have to work for it. In 2 Thessalonians 3:10–12 Paul says that Christians must 'work in quietness and eat their own bread'. He also says, 'If anyone will not work, neither shall he eat.'

But for the Christian there is more purpose in work than just that. Whether you are a college student, a housewife or a professional earning your living, your daily work should be service for Jesus Christ. It is a great mistake to think that your service for him is only your spare time Christian activity and that your day's work is merely the wearisome business of paying the bills. To separate your life into two compartments, sacred and secular, is unbiblical and is thoroughly dishonouring to Jesus Christ. He is our heavenly Master and we are in his service all day long, seven days a week. We must therefore learn to do everything as part of our service for him. In Colossians 3:23 Paul exhorts, 'Whatever you do, do it heartily, as to the Lord and not to men.'

So if you are a student, you need to learn diligently for Christ. These years of educational opportunity will likely never come again, and if you make the most of them now, your life will be more useful to God later. Or, if you are a woman and God has given you the privilege of marriage and a family, your work is in your home looking after your husband and training your children. Christian mothers are the most influential people in the world. Your prayers, example and teaching may not only lead your children to trust Christ, but through them it can also reach out to others.

Again, if you are an employer or an employee, it does not matter whether you are producing food, building homes, defending your country or healing the sick, you are not just earning a wage. You are working with God for the physical, mental, emotional and spiritual development of his creatures. This is his will for all of us. God's purpose for us while we are on earth is not just that we be saved. God wants us also to grow into balanced, healthy, happy, educated and useful people whose lives bring glory and honour to him. Every honourable employment fits somewhere into this picture, be it in one of the professions, business, industry or entertainment. Therefore every Christian ought to see himself working hand in hand with God. And he or she ought to have no greater incentive than to do that job 'as to the Lord, and not unto men' (Eph. 6:7).

4. Playing

As the old proverb says, 'All work and no play makes Jack a dull boy.' Or as someone else has said, 'People who cannot find time for recreation, are obliged sooner or later to find time for illness.' Leisure is indispensable for the overall health of body and mind. The real problem with our leisure time is not choosing what to do, but how to keep others from using it. Leisure, of course, should be balanced. It should cater to the mind and the body. But whatever it is, we need to take time off for leisure. Did not our Lord say, 'Come aside by yourselves to a deserted place and rest awhile' (Mark 6:31)? And Solomon speaks of 'a time to weep, and a time to laugh; a time to mourn, and a time to dance' (Eccles. 3:4).

Now having said that we need to spend time on ourselves (sleeping, eating, working and playing), it is important to state that these things are to remain our servants and not become our masters. There will be occasions when we will be called on to spend time on

God and others that normally we would spend on ourselves. There will be times when we will have to cut sleep to nurse a sick loved one, or cut food so that we can fast and pray to God. But notwithstanding these, it is perfectly valid to spend time on ourselves.

Important demands by others on our time

Another area to consider is the demands that others — family, church, community — place on our time.

1. Our family

To support the home financially is not enough. Our children need more than food and drink, clothes and shelter. They need instruction as well (and not just in the three Rs at school). They need to be instructed in the things of life, to be taught the Word of God and Christian standards and values. They need time to be prepared for marriage and family life. They need time to discuss their personal problems with us, share their views with us, and be with us and enjoy leisure together.

These are all vital elements in the process of providing for our children's full development. We owe it to them to give them this time and thought. Children are not pets to be enjoyed —

they are people who need to be prepared for life. That is the responsibility we take on when we have a family. Of course, let us not forget our spouse. Our husband or wife ought to come first, even before our children. A spouse is not to be taken for granted and it is important to set aside time to be alone and to go out alone with our spouse. Your spouse wants more than the month's wages or a good meal. Your spouse wants you — and one of your wedding vows was to 'love and cherish' your spouse.

2. Our church

One of the great dangers in church life is attending meetings on almost every day or night of the week that serve no other purpose than to promote a department of the church and its program. These meetings can take up valuable time but contribute very little to our spiritual growth or the advancement of the gospel.

So when we say we are to give time to the church, we do not mean giving time to regularly attend all sorts of meetings that do not focus on fellowship with one another in prayer and Bible study. Christ's church is not a club whose members get together to enjoy each other's company in fruitless activity. Rather, it is a fellowship of God's people whose joy it is to build each other up for evangelism and good works through studying God's Word together, praying together and exhorting and comforting one another. This will not only involve time for attending the midweek Bible study and prayer meeting, besides the services on the Lord's Day, but also for visiting one another or communicating with one another by telephone, email or letter.

3. Our community

We are not to confine our time only to our home and our church. The community in which we live also has a claim on our lives and what we have to offer. It may be visiting the sick or the elderly or the prisoner. It may be giving assistance to the poor or guidance to the confused. It may be rehabilitating addicts or rescuing the suicidal. There are many ways in which our community can benefit from our time. We need to seek the Lord's face as to where our time can be best invested. But make it a spiritual involvement. As Jesus said, 'Follow me, and let the dead bury their own dead' (Matt. 8:22). There are responsibilities to our community that can be adequately met by the spiritually dead. Use your time to further God's kingdom in your community.

Spending time on God himself

As I have already indicated, time for ourselves and time for others is also time for God. But this must never become a substitute for spending time on God himself. The Bible demands from beginning to end that we should spend time on God. We can do this in the following ways.

1. In public

Why do we have a midweek meeting? Why do we have two services on a Sunday? The answer is that we want to give time to God himself. We want to publicly worship God and bring glory to him through our praise, prayer and meditation. Many people today, however, seek a church home purely on the grounds of their own perceived interests as opposed to God's revealed will in Scripture. Their criteria for choosing a church is: Does it have a good choir? Is the children's program captivating? Are there many teenagers in the youth group, and are they friendly? Does the church conduct its worship services in an informal way and sing contemporary Christian songs? Does the preacher speak in a conversational manner? Will the worship inspire me and lift me up for the week? Some people will not attend a church unless they can get pumped up emotionally in the services.

What we need to realize is that 'Man's chief end is to glorify God, and to enjoy him for ever', as the *Westminster Shorter Catechism* says. Not only that, we need to see more clearly than ever that worship is only glorifying to God when it is evoked by the Spirit of God through the Word of God. Expository biblical preaching is far more vital to God-honouring worship than an entertaining program of music and drama together with other gimmicks to create excitement and good feelings about ourselves.

So the greatest use to which we can put our time in the public worship of God is to sit under the faithful ministry of his Word. To put it another way, submitting

EXPLANATION

to what God has to say to us through Holy Scripture has priority over what we have to say to him in prayer and praise. Both are forms of giving worship to God and he delights in them both, but the former is even more glorifying to him than the latter. The words in 1 Samuel 15:22 are quite explicit:

> Has the Lord as great delight in burnt
>   offerings and sacrifices,
>   As in obeying the voice of the Lord?
> Behold, to obey is better than sacrifice,
>   And to heed than the fat of rams.

Now to give time to worshipping God every Sunday morning and evening is not asking for much, is it? It is something we should delight in — something we cannot get enough of. As the Scripture says,

> If you turn away your foot from the
>   Sabbath,
> From doing your pleasure on my holy day,
> And call the Sabbath a delight,
> The holy day of the Lord honorable,
> And shall honor him, not doing your own
>   ways,
> Nor finding your own pleasure,
> Nor speaking your own words,
> Then you shall delight yourself in the
>   Lord;

And I will cause you to ride on the high hills of
    the earth,
And feed you with the heritage of Jacob your father.
The mouth of the Lord has spoken
(Isa. 58:13–14).

That is how our Lord spent his Sabbaths (Luke 4:16).
It is true that the Bible does not say how many times
on a Sunday we should meet for worship, but surely
Sunday is the Lord's Day and not ours? And so we
should take advantage of this day to immerse ourselves
in the worship and the Word of God.

This has been the conviction of Christians for century
after century: the best way to use the Lord's Day is to
begin and *end* it together in the Lord's house worshipping him. Indeed, so strong has been this instinct, that
for the first 400 years when Sunday was not an official
day of rest, the early church gathered for worship early
in the morning before they went to work and then late
at night when their work was done (Acts 20:7–12). We
would soon find out who the Lord's people are today if
we had to worship at those hours because we had to go
to work every Sunday.

And then again, where did we ever get the idea that
it is improper for a service to go on for longer than sixty
minutes? Do we imagine that that is about as much as
God can endure? Or would it be more truthful to say
that sixty minutes is all our selfish hearts are prepared
to give him? Although all our time belongs to God, he still
demands one day out of seven exclusively for himself.
Not one hour but one day. Let me say in the strongest

terms that to spend the Lord's Day on ourselves is as bad as spending the tithe on ourselves. It is robbing God of what is his, and stolen time is ill-gained. As Sir Matthew Hale put it:

A Sunday well spent
Brings a week of content,
And health for the toils of tomorrow;
But a Sabbath profaned,
Whatever be gained,
Is a certain forerunner of sorrow.

It is our duty to spend time in *public* on God. But that, important as it is, is not enough. We need to spend time on God in private.

2. In private
If you really love someone, you long to be alone with that person. It is nice being with the whole family, but we do look forward to being alone with our spouse. Well, the same is true of God. If we really love God we will also desire to have some time alone with him. We will want to spend time in private prayer and communion with God every day. We will want to spend time reading systematically through the Bible because it is there that God has revealed his will for us as individual believers, for his church and for all creation.

To do this properly and beneficially will require time to meditate on the portion of Scripture we

EXPLANATION

have read for that day. Take time to ask yourself: What is God saying to me through these words? Do they apply to a specific area of my life? If so, am I obeying them (1 Sam. 15:22)? If not, am I ready to confess my disobedience, repent of it and ask God's forgiveness through Christ? Is there some truth about God in these verses that can deepen my love for him or strengthen my faith in him? Sometimes we will need to spend time reading a commentary that can help us better understand the passage of Scripture we are reading. Time spent alone with God every day is one of the greatest means of blessing in our Christian lives. Through it we can learn more about the hideousness and pervasiveness of the remaining sin in us and the amazing greatness and goodness of the God who saves us from it.

What a vital commodity this is which God has entrusted to us! No wonder the apostle Paul speaks about 'redeeming the time' (Eph. 5:16). The Greek word means 'to buy up', and it was used in the marketplace. It is the kind of phrase that you might use for buying up the entire stock of a valuable commodity that is in short supply. And, of course, for the Christian, time is just such a precious commodity. The stock is limited and it must be bought in the face of keen competition from the world, the flesh and the devil. It must be bought for our heavenly Father, says Bishop Moule, 'at the expense of self-denying watchfulness'. It will not do to let things drift because 'the days are evil' (Eph. 5:15, NIV). That is to say, our days in a sinful world do not lend themselves to holy pursuits. Satan wants to see every minute misused. It is up to us to make every minute count for God.

Are we 'redeeming the time'? Are we making the most of it? Are we buying up every precious, scarce minute? We often say, 'If you take care of the pennies/cents, the pounds/dollars will take care of themselves.' Well, the same is true of our time: 'Take care of the *hours* and the *days* will take care of themselves.' Are we then watching the hours and the minutes? Have we ever looked at a schedule of our daily lives to see if we are wasting time? Perhaps it would be wise if we did.

THINK ABOUT IT

Time is not yours to dispose of as you please; it is a glorious talent that men must be accountable for as well as any other talent.
— *Thomas Brooks*

We live by demands when we should live by priorities.
— *J. A. Motyer*

We give so little thought to the fact that God made time as a preparation for eternity, and this earth the place where we acquire our entry either to heaven or hell.
— *Spiros Zodhiates*

Now there will be a great temptation here to agree by and large with what has been said so far in this chapter and not examine our daily and weekly schedule to see if we may be misspending this precious God-given resource of time. That would be sheer folly for it would simply result in the continued misuse of our time. The wise thing to do, if we want to redeem the time we are currently wasting, would be for us to draw up a weekly schedule of how we are presently spending our time.

Without being legalistic or too restrictive, let us write down in round figures the hours we spend on meals, sleep, work (including travel time there and back), recreation for ourselves and our family, daily personal prayer and Bible reading, family devotions, Sunday worship services and a midweek meeting for corporate prayer and Bible study. How many hours do we have left? This will vary from person to person according to their age, needs and legitimate duties. Everyone, however, will have some time left that ought not to be wasted on selfish, useless pursuits, time that could be used instead to serve God and our fellow man in some practical way (like teaching in Sunday school, visiting the sick and homebound, counselling the distressed, encouraging the saints or winning the lost).

Is that what we are doing? Are we spending these extra hours every week on things that count for God and eternity? Jesus said, 'But I say to you that for every idle word men may speak, they will give account of it in the day of judgement' (Matt. 12:36). The same goes, of course, for every idle minute we waste. Time is a commodity that ultimately belongs to God. We need, therefore, to learn to pray with the psalmist: 'So teach us to number our days, that we may gain a heart of wisdom' (Ps. 90:12). We need a heart that will put our few remaining days to the highest possible use.

Here, as in every other area of our life, our Lord Jesus Christ is our supreme example. He knew that his Father had a plan for his life just as God has a plan for the lives of all his children. He could say, 'My food is to do the will of him who sent me, and to finish his work' (John 4:34). And we can say with Paul that we have been 'created in Christ Jesus for good works, which God prepared beforehand that we should walk in them' (Eph. 2:10). If this is true, the corollary is that there are enough hours in each day for us to fulfil God's perfect and particular plan for every day of our lives.

Follow our Lord's life through the Gospels. Thronged by demanding crowds, Jesus was never in a hurry. Time held no power over him. On several occasions he asserted that his hour had not yet come, and implicit in this assertion was the consciousness that his Father's plan had been drawn up with such meticulous accuracy that every hour was accounted for and designed to achieve the divine purpose for his life.

His schedule had been arranged, and his sole concern on earth was to fulfil the work that had been given to him to do in the allotted hours (John 7:6; 12:23,27; 13:1; 17:1). Jesus would not even allow his much-loved mother to interfere with this divinely planned timetable (John 2:4).

Nor would he allow his deep affection for Martha and Mary to move up his schedule by two days because his Father's plan to be glorified in the resurrection of their brother Lazarus would be marred (John 11:6,9). It is not surprising then, that at the end of his earthly life Jesus could declare, 'I have glorified you on the earth. I have finished the work which you have given me to do' (John 17:4).

It is easy, of course, to stand afar off and admire in our Lord these desirable traits that so often are lacking in our own lives. But Jesus is to be followed and imitated, not only admired. We have the same Holy Spirit who indwelt him to help us. Thus Paul says, 'See then that you walk circumspectly [that is, like a cat walking on the top of a concrete wall embedded with pieces of glass, watching carefully where it puts each paw], not as fools but as wise, redeeming the time, because the days are evil. Therefore, do not be unwise, but understand what the will of the Lord is' (Eph. 5:15–17). And where are we going to get the wisdom to know the will of the Lord and the strength to do it? Paul immediately goes on to tell us: 'And do not be drunk with wine, in which is dissipation; but be filled with the Spirit' (Eph. 5:18). In other words, be controlled and influenced by the Holy Spirit, just as a drunk man is controlled and influenced by wine. For the Spirit will show us the will of God and enable us to do it.

Do not say that you do not have the time or that you are too busy. When we talk like that we have either taken on responsibilities not laid on us by the Lord or we are not making strategic use of the time he has given us. Each of us has as much time as anyone else in the world. As in the parable of the pounds or minas in Luke 19, we are each entrusted with the same amount of time but we do not all use it profitably to produce a tenfold return. The mina, you see, represents the resource we hold in trust for God, and in this parable time would be a good example of what our Lord had in mind. For as each servant was given one mina, so each one of us is given the same hours each day to use for God. But the servant who used his mina to earn ten more for his master was given a greater reward than the servant who used his mina to earn an additional five. Why? His reward was greater because the first servant put his time/resource to greater use than the second servant or any of the others. This is sobering indeed. The use we make of our time on earth for God is going to have eternal consequences.

Let us heed the advice of a few great men from the past:

> Spend your time in nothing which you know must be repented of; in nothing on which you might not pray for the blessing of God; in nothing which you could not review with a quiet conscience on your dying bed; in nothing which you might not safely and properly be found doing if death should surprise you in the act.
> — *Richard Baxter*

I am not careful for what may be a hundred years hence. He who governed the world before I was born shall take care of it likewise when I am dead. My part is to improve the present moment.
— *John Wesley*

Live so as to be missed.
— *Robert Murray M'Cheyne*

Let us be faithful stewards of the time God has put in our charge for what we weave in time we wear in eternity. As we seek to faithfully serve our Master, Jesus Christ, let us not be panicked in any way, but take comfort in the words of Thomas Fuller: 'Man is immortal till his work is done.'

KEY THOUGHTS

To spend time on purely selfish pursuits is a crime in God's eyes. It robs God, our fellow men and our very selves of much service of eternal benefit. We are not our own but have been bought at a price — no less than the precious blood of Jesus Christ. As the only wise God, our Saviour, it is his will that we give the right amount of time to all our God-given responsibilities on earth. This requires wisdom and resolve that in our fallen condition we do not have. Our duty therefore is to keep on being filled with the Holy Spirit, who alone can help us to buy up whatever moments of this scarce commodity we have left and use them for the glory of God and the good of all men, especially the household of faith. Inaction will prove disastrous.

QUESTIONS FOR DISCUSSION

DISCUSS IT

1. *Spiros Zodhiates once said, 'God made time as a preparation for eternity.' Discuss or consider this statement and give biblical references to support your reasons for agreeing or not agreeing with it.*

2. *Read Proverbs 6:6–11 and 24:30–34 and draw from these passages the lessons God intends us to learn.*

3. *What do you think is the connecting line of thought in Ephesians 5:15–21?*

4. *As a practical help, do a breakdown of how your time is currently spent:*
   a. *How much time do you spend on work and study, sleep, eating and leisure?*
   b. *How much time do you spend on spouse and family, your local church and your community?*
   c. *How much time do you spend on Sunday services, midweek prayer and Bible study and private devotions?*
   d. *Of the remaining hours each week, is there any-thing you are spending too much time on?*
   e. *If God called you now to account for the use of your time, would you be happy or ashamed of your stewardship?*

SUGGESTIONS FOR PRAYER

1. *Ask God in his mercy to forgive you for all the time you have wasted on selfish and worthless pursuits.*

2. *Acknowledge your utter dependence on his Spirit for wisdom and power to correct your misuse of time.*

3. *Pray that God will fill you with his Spirit as you yield yourself afresh to him.*

Faith of our fathers! living still
    In spite of dungeon, fire, and sword;
O how our hearts beat high with joy
    Whene'er we hear that glorious word.

Our Fathers, chained in prisons dark,
    Were still in heart and conscience free:
And blest would be their children's fate,
    Though they, like them, should die for thee.

Faith of our fathers! God's great power
    Shall soon all nations win for thee;
And through the truth that comes from God
    Mankind shall then be truly free.

Faith of our fathers! we will love
    Both friend and foe in all our strife,
And preach thee too, as love knows how,
    By kindly words and virtuous life;

    Faith of our fathers, holy faith,
    We will be true to thee till death.

— Frederick W. Faber (1814–1863)

CHAPTER SEVEN

THE
STEWARDSHIP
OF OUR
FAITH

LOOK IT UP

BIBLE REFERENCE

O Timothy! Guard what was committed to your trust,
avoiding the profane and idle babblings
and contradictions of what is falsely called knowledge
— by professing it, some have strayed
concerning the faith
(1 Tim. 6:20–21).

INTRODUCTION

The doctrine of Christian stewardship is not dealt with in books on systematic theology, even though it is of great practical importance to every believer as they seek to fulfil the purpose of his or her high calling in Christ Jesus. Although we are not saved by the good works that we do, we have been saved to live a life of good works — for these bring glory to God and blessing to others, especially the 'household of faith'. In Ephesians 2:8–10 Paul says,

For by grace you have been saved through faith, and that not of yourselves; it is the gift of God, not of works, lest anyone should boast. For we are his workmanship, created in Christ Jesus for good works, which God prepared beforehand that we should walk in them.

The Bible is full of the subject of stewardship. As we have seen in earlier chapters, God has no children who are not also stewards of the goods he has entrusted to them for the benefit of his people. So far we have considered our responsibility to be faithful trustees and dispensers of the body, the mind, the talents and the time that God has placed in our care. In this chapter we come to another of our Master's goods that we are to faithfully dispense to the church and the world, and that is 'the faith which was once for all delivered to the saints' (Jude 3).

The gospel and Scripture are often spoken of in this way. They are seen as the body of truth that has been handed down to all humankind by Jesus Christ through his prophets in the Old Testament and his apostles in the New. In 1 Corinthians 16:13 Paul tells us to 'stand fast in the faith'. In 2 Corinthians 13:5 he commands us to 'examine yourselves as to whether you are in the faith'. In Colossians 1:23 we are to 'continue in the faith'. In 1 Timothy 6:21 we are told of some who 'have strayed concerning the faith'. And in Revelation 2:13 Jesus commends the Christians in Pergamos because 'you hold fast to my name, and did not deny my faith'.

Now it is true that those whom God has called to be pastors and teachers in the church are the chief stewards of God's truth. Thus in Titus 1:7–9 Paul says that 'a bishop [or elder] must be blameless, as a steward of God... holding fast the faithful word as he has been taught, that he may be able, by sound doctrine, both to exhort and convict those who contradict [the truth]'. The apostle says a similar thing in 1 Corinthians 4:1, 'Let a man so consider us, as servants of Christ and stewards of the mysteries of God.' Paul is referring to himself and

Apollos as itinerant preachers, and the goods over which they have been appointed as stewards are called 'the mysteries of God'. The Greek word for mystery here does not mean some dark, unexplained enigma but the truth once hidden that God has now made known through his prophets and apostles. So 'the mysteries of God' refer to the sum of his self-revelation as revealed in Scripture. And every preacher is a steward, charged with the task of making biblical truths known and understood in God's household.

But as we have seen before, every Christian is also a steward of God and is not exempt from the responsibility of dispensing God's Word. For example, the words in Jude 20 — 'building yourselves up on your most holy faith' — are addressed to all the members of the church. Indeed, in Ephesians 4:11–14 Paul says that Christ has given to the church 'pastors and teachers, for the equipping of the saints for the work of the ministry, for the edifying of the body of Christ, till we all come to... the knowledge of the Son of God... that we should no longer be children, tossed to and fro... with every wind of doctrine, by the trickery of men'. In other words, spiritual immaturity leads to gullibility. As children are easily taken in or tricked by deceitful people, so God's purpose is that pastors and teachers are to equip every member in the church and help them to be built up and become mature in their faith.

God's Word, however, is not just for the building up
of the saints, it is also to be the means whereby the
church saves the lost. Thus Jude tells us to be 'building
yourselves up on your most holy faith... but others save
with fear, pulling them out of the fire' (Jude 20,23).
The church is both a *worshipping* and a *witnessing*
community. In fact, our duty to witness to Christ is the
only reason why we are not glorified and taken to heaven
the moment we are converted. After all, if we were
saved just to worship God, why would he leave us on
earth when all our worship here could be done better in
heaven? Surely the only answer is that God has left us
here as witnesses to win more true worshippers of him.
Unbelievers are on their way to hell where they will
never glorify God. Their life in eternity will be spent in
cursing the God who made them and loves them. So
Jude says to all Christians, 'others save with fear,
pulling them out of the fire'. Worship without witness
is as dead as 'faith without works' (James 2:20).

With that lengthy but necessary explanation, let us now
look at what the stewardship of our faith involves. Paul
writes, 'Moreover it is required in stewards that one be
found faithful' (1 Cor. 4:2). And there are two main areas
of faithfulness required in our stewardship of the faith.

We are to be faithful
to our Master himself

As we have seen, God's Word is a sacred trust that has
been committed to all believers. Paul writes of this

several times in his epistles. In 1 Thessalonians 2:4 he says, 'But as we have been approved by God to be entrusted with the gospel, even so we speak, not as pleasing men, but God who tests our hearts.' As stewards our primary responsibility is to please God by faithfully doing the task he has entrusted to us. Thus Paul can say to the Corinthians, 'For if I preach the gospel, I have nothing to boast of, for necessity is laid upon me; yes, woe is me if I do not preach the gospel! For... I have been entrusted with a stewardship' (1 Cor. 9:16–17).

But the clearest way the apostle expresses our responsibility to God is in Romans 1:14–16. Having introduced himself to his readers as a bondservant of Jesus Christ, Paul continues,

> I am a debtor both to Greeks and to barbarians, both to wise and to unwise. So, as much as is in me, I am ready to preach the gospel to you who are in Rome also. For I am not ashamed of the gospel of Christ, for it is the power of God to salvation for everyone who believes.

Paul saw himself as 'a debtor' because of the gospel. What did he mean? How could the gospel be a debt that he owed?

Well, there are two possible ways of getting into debt. The first is to borrow money *from* someone, and the second is to be given money *for* someone. For example, if I borrowed $1,000 from you I would be in your debt until I paid it back. Equally, if a relative of yours were to hand me $1,000 to give to you I would be in your debt until I handed it over. It is in this second sense that Paul is in debt. He has not borrowed anything from the Romans that he must repay, but Jesus Christ had entrusted him with the gospel *for* them, and therefore Paul was in debt to the Romans.

Now what was true of Paul is true of all Christians. We are debtors to the world, even though we are not apostles. If the gospel has come to us (which it has), we are not at liberty to keep it to ourselves. No person or group may claim a monopoly on the gospel. Good news is for sharing. We are under an obligation to make it known to others. This was the incentive for Paul's faithful stewardship of the gospel. A steward has received a trust and he must show himself worthy of this trust. Teaching and witnessing are hard work and we will often be tempted to become discouraged. We need this powerful incentive to strengthen our flagging zeal — *our heavenly Father is depending on us.* The rest of his household are looking to us for the provisions that he has entrusted to us. We must not fail to fulfil our trust and discharge our debt. Rather, may our response be, in the words of Charles Wesley:

My talents, gifts and graces, Lord,
   Into Thy blessed hands receive;
And let me live to preach Thy Word
   And let me to Thy glory live;
My every sacred moment spend
   In publishing the sinner's Friend.

We are to be faithful to those who look to us for sustenance

In 1 Peter 4:10 the apostle is speaking to all Christians when he says, 'As each one has received a gift, minister it to one another, as good stewards of the manifold grace of God.' He then goes on to say, 'If anyone speaks, let him speak as the oracles of God' (1 Peter 4:11). The Greek word *logia* translated here as oracles means words, and it refers to the Scriptures. Peter is saying that when Christians speak as the stewards of God, their messages are to be words spoken by God himself. To put it another way, their teaching is to be true to Scripture.

The gospel or the Christian faith is a sacred stewardship that has been given to us, not for our own benefit but for the blessing of God's household at large. The Christian, therefore, must neither hoard nor waste the goods that his Master has committed to his trust. He must dispense God's Word to the whole household. In order to do this, two things will be required of the Christian: diligence in dispensing the truth and knowledge of the people being instructed.

1. Diligence in dispensing all the truth to the household
The metaphor of stewardship teaches us very clearly that we do not supply our own message. Rather, it is the message that God has already

given to us in his Word. Just as a steward is not expected to feed the household out of his own resources, neither is the Christian teacher to provide a message from his own imagination. There are a few New Testament metaphors that elaborate on this fact. The Christian is a *sower* of seed and 'the seed is the Word of God' according to Luke 8:11. The Christian is also a *herald*, and the herald is instructed by the ruler what good news he is to announce (1 Cor. 1:23; 2 Cor. 4:5). The Christian is a *builder* helping to erect a temple for God, but both the foundation and the materials to build on it have already been provided (1 Cor. 3:9–15). To quote Jude 20 again, 'But you, beloved, building yourselves up on your most holy faith.'

The church, therefore, is not to be a place for political speculation or social debate. It is God's house and we are to feed his people on the Word of God and nothing else. Paul stresses this point to Timothy: 'O Timothy! Guard what was committed to your trust, avoiding the profane and vain babblings and contradictions of what is falsely called knowledge — by professing it, some have strayed concerning the faith' (1 Tim. 6:20–21). In 1 Timothy 1:11 Paul calls it 'the glorious gospel of the blessed God' which has been committed to our care. So we must stand guard over it like watchmen guarding a city. We must not allow ourselves or anyone else to 'adulterate the Word of God' (2 Cor. 4:2, NASB) or 'twist to their own destruction... the Scriptures' (2 Peter 3:16).

Moreover, Paul could say to the church at Ephesus, 'I am innocent of the blood of all men. For I have not shunned to declare to you the whole counsel of God'

166

THE GUIDE

EXPLANATION

(Acts 20:26–27). Paul recognized, as he says in Colossians 1:25, that 'the stewardship from God... was given to me for your benefit, to present to you the Word of God in its fulness'. How many of us can claim to be that faithful to God and his Word? Whether we are parents, Sunday school teachers, youth workers, counsellors or preachers, we tend to stick to our favourite doctrines. We pick and choose from the Scriptures, selecting the passages we like and passing over those we dislike or find difficult. If we do not like doctrines like the eternal punishment of the wicked or the predestination of God's elect or the total depravity of all humanity, we simply omit them from our curriculum. And by doing so we deprive God's household of important truth that our Master has deemed absolutely essential for their eternal spiritual welfare.

But if some fail in their stewardship of the faith by *subtracting* from Scripture, others are tempted to go to the opposite extreme of *adding* to the biblical revelation. Nothing more is to be added because the faith has been 'once for all delivered to the saints' (Jude 3). Any additions like baptismal regeneration, salvation by works, sinless perfection or the infallibility of the pope are all human embellishments — inherently erroneous and spiritually harmful to our fellow servants.

However, the worst offence that we can commit in regards to 'the truth [that] is in Jesus' (Eph.

4:21) is to *contradict* it, such as to claim that the Bible endorses homosexuality, abortion, euthanasia, prayers for the dead or universal salvation (the belief that everyone is going to heaven in the end). Such teaching can only result in the spiritual destruction of those who hold it.

No householder who loves his household would tolerate such flagrant disregard of his orders. If a house-holder issues milk, bread, meat, fruit and vegetables to his steward with instructions to dispense them to the members of the household in suitable portions each day, he expects his orders to be diligently carried out. If, however, his steward has his own idea of what the members of the household need or would like and decides to disregard his master's orders and treat the household to as much ice cream as they want, that would be a flat *contradiction* of his master's orders. His master would not be pleased to say the least.

Again, if the steward decided to give them milk, bread and fruit but not meat and vegetables, he would still be derelict in his duty. He would be *subtracting* essential items from the household's diet, and his master would once again not be very happy with him. Or if he should decide to give them milk, bread, meat, vegetables and fruit, plus some cake, he would be *adding* something that is not nutritious to the well-planned diet of his mas-ter. Once more he would incur his master's displeasure. What must the steward do to make his master happy? He must obey his orders and give the household *exactly* what he has been issued to give them. He must give them nothing else, nothing less and nothing more. This is faithfulness and that is what Paul says is required in stewards of the mysteries of God.

We live in a day when the church urgently needs stewards who will faithfully dispense the whole counsel of God (Acts 20:20,27) — not just the New Testament but the Old as well, not just the most comforting texts but also the most challenging, not just the passages that favour our particular interpretation of Scripture but also those that do not. Some churches go over and over the doctrines of grace, the gifts of the Holy Spirit, or the second coming of Christ, instead of systematically expounding every part of God's Word. I like our Lord's picture of a steward in Matthew 13. Jesus says to his disciples, 'It has been given to you to know the mysteries of the kingdom of heaven', and then he goes on to say that every disciple is 'like a householder [or housekeeper] who brings out of his treasure things new and old' (Matt. 13:11,52).

In a world of religious pluralism, only faithful exposition of Scripture will enable believers to discern what has been divinely revealed and what has not. Moreover, only by adhering to God's Word will we have the courage to be dogmatic about what is plain and at the same time be content to leave unknown what is still shrouded in mystery. The spirit of Philip Henry is worthy of emulation: 'In those things in which all the people of God are agreed, I will spend my zeal; and as for other things about which they differ,

I will walk according to the light God hath given me, and charitably believe that others do so too.'

THINK ABOUT IT

Jesus saw himself as the key to scripture and it as the key to himself.
— *J. I. Packer*

It is more to God's glory that the world should be conquered by the force of truth than by the blaze of miracles.
— *C. H. Spurgeon*

The Christian preacher is to be neither a speculator who invents new doctrines which please him, nor an editor who excises old doctrines which displease him, but a steward, God's steward, dispensing faithfully to God's household the truths committed to him in the Scriptures, nothing more, nothing less and nothing else.
— *John R. W. Stott*

The Scripture is both the breeder and feeder of grace.
— *Thomas Watson*

Generally speaking, evangelical churches in America are theologically conservative but biblically illiterate. That is why moderates and liberals made such inroads into mainline Protestant churches during the twentieth century. Sunday school literature is often skimpy and repetitious, and the preaching is increasingly focused on solving practical personal problems. The following advertisement for a series of sermons is a good example:

Don't miss this practical series!
'The Fundamentals of Financial Freedom'
October 7 — 'Will I ever have enough?'
October 14 — 'How to Diffuse the Debt Bomb'
October 21 — 'The secret of praying for
    your needs'
October 28 — 'Why you should become a
    generous person'

EXPLANATION

The contemporary preoccupation with sermons on financial troubles, marital problems, parenting, depression or personal relationships is increasingly alarming. Evangelical churches in English-speaking countries are becoming too man centred and less and less God centred.

The church today desperately needs members who know what the Bible teaches and are 'ready to give a defence to everyone who asks [them] a reason for the hope that is in [them]' (1 Peter 3:15). Nothing can bring about this happy result except the solid, systematic and faithful teaching of the entire Word of God. And such conscientious teaching is not possible without disciplined learning. As long as church members do not regularly avail themselves of the teaching that is offered to them on Sundays and mid-week, they will remain uninformed and unable to teach others.

Let us heed the searching words of Richard Baxter to his congregation at Kidderminster where he ministered for over forty years. He said,

Were you but as willing to get the knowledge of God and heavenly things as you are to know how to work in your trade, you would have set yourself to it before this day, and you would have spared no cost or pains till you had got it. But you account seven years little enough to learn your trade, and will not bestow one day in seven in diligent learning the matters of your salvation.

2. A knowledge of the people he is instructing

A wise steward varies the diet that he gives to his master's household. He studies their needs and uses his discretion in supplying them with suitable food. The steward has no say in determining what goes into the larder or pantry — it is stocked for him by the master. But it is the steward's responsibility to decide what comes out of it and when and in what measure. As Jesus says in Luke 12:42, 'Who then is that faithful and wise steward, whom his master will make ruler over his household, to give them their portion of food in due season?' There will be babies in the household and children, as well as adults and the elderly. The infants will require milk and finely mashed vegetables and fruit. The steward, therefore, must take pains to make the food appetizing for children who have not yet acquired a taste for cabbage or spinach or any other new and healthy vegetables.

EXPLANATION

The steward's wisdom and faithfulness, then, will be displayed in the balance and suitability of the diet that he gives to each member of the household. Likewise, every steward of God must show similar wisdom and faithfulness towards the 'household of faith'. Paul had to deal with this issue at Corinth and he took measures to correct their spiritual diet by rebuking their worldliness. He says,

And I, brethren, could not speak to you as to spiritual people but as to carnal [literally, fleshly people], as to babes in Christ. I fed you with milk and not with solid food; for until now you were not able to receive it, and even now you are still not able; for you are still carnal (1 Cor. 3:1–3).

The writer of Hebrews also encountered this problem. In Hebrews 5:11–14 he writes,

We have much to say, and hard to explain, since you have become dull of hearing. For though by this time you ought to be teachers, you need someone to teach you again the first principles of the oracles of God; and you have come to need milk and not solid food. For everyone who partakes only of milk is unskilled in the word of righteousness, for he is a babe. But solid food belongs to those who are of full age, that is, those

who by reason of use have their senses exercised
[or trained] to discern both good and evil.

So, when faced with such a situation a faithful steward
will not falsify God's Word in order to make it more
appealing. Neither will he dilute the strong medicine
of Scripture (its words of rebuke) to make it sweeter to
the taste. His duty is to make God's Word as simple and
direct as possible.

In Paul's words to Timothy, a steward must be 'diligent... a worker who does not need to be ashamed,
rightly dividing the word of truth' (2 Tim. 2:15). The
Greek word translated as rightly dividing means literally cutting straight. It was used in reference to the
building of roads and it occurs in the Greek version of
Proverbs 3:6: 'He will make your paths straight'
(NASB). Our teaching of Scripture — at home, in
church and on the mission field — is to be so simple
and direct that it is as easy to follow as a straight road.
It must be like the 'Highway of Holiness' in Isaiah 35:8
where it is said, 'Whoever walks the road, although a
fool, shall not go astray.'

But as I pointed out at the beginning, God's Word
is not just for current members of God's household
but also for those who are yet to be added to it. Our
Lord Jesus Christ says in John 10:16, 'And other
sheep I have which are not of this fold; them also I
must bring, and they will hear my voice; and there
will be one flock and one shepherd.' And just before
he ascended into heaven Jesus commissioned his
disciples, saying,

EXPLANATION

All authority has been given to me in heaven and on earth. Go therefore and make disciples of all the nations, baptizing them in the name of the Father and of the Son and of the Holy Spirit, teaching them to observe all things that I have commanded you; and lo, I am with you always, even to the end of the age (Matt. 28:18–20).

The Word, therefore, is not to be confined to the household of faith but shared with the rest of the world. 'For it is the power of God to salvation for everyone who believes' (Rom. 1:16) and 'the word of life' that begets eternal life in every sinner who obeys it and receives Christ as their Saviour (Phil. 2:16; John 3:36). In the parable in Luke 14:16–24 God's stewards are commanded to invite outsiders to come and dine at the Master's table: 'Compel them to come in, that my house may be filled.' Again, Christians are commanded in Philippians 2:15–16 to 'hold out the word of life' to 'a crooked and depraved generation' (NIV). The word 'hold out' was often used in classical Greek to mean offering something to somebody, especially in reference to holding out food or drink to a guest while serving them a meal. What is very remarkable is that Paul goes on in verse 16 to state the reason for this command: 'so that I may rejoice in the day of Christ that I have not run in vain or laboured in vain' (NKJV). In other words, if the Christians at Philippi did not offer to their friends and neighbours the Word that brings eternal life, Paul would regard his work of discipling them as having been wasted. Isn't that an extraordinary statement to make? The apostle regarded witnessing to Christ at home and abroad as an essential part of our Christian life and our service to God.

When the early Christians were persecuted in Jerusalem, Luke says that 'they were all scattered throughout the regions of Judea and Samaria... therefore those who were scattered went everywhere preaching the word' (Acts 8:1,4). Every Christian was in the business of witnessing to the unsaved. Why? Because before Christ's ascension he gave this charge: 'Go... and make disciples of all the nations' (Matt. 28:19). It is a commission that is binding on every member of the church. And though we are not all called to be pastors or missionaries, every Christian is called to be a witness to Christ in the particular locality in which God in his sovereignty has placed him or her. Indeed, this kind of personal evangelism has a value that in some respects is not possible when we are publicly preaching the gospel. In private witness the message can be adapted more personally to the particular person to whom we are speaking, as Jesus did with the woman at Jacob's well and with Nicodemus.

Now some Christians make the mistake of supposing that God intends them to speak of Christ to everyone they meet. It is a very laudable goal, but the demands of such a widespread ministry are so heavy that very few, if any, could fulfil them. Although we must witness whenever God gives us the opportunity to do so, the best way to try and win others to Christ is to begin by

EXPLANATION

praying that God would lay on our hearts a burden for a few unconverted people on whom we can concentrate our efforts. As soon as someone is laid on our hearts we must try to win their friendship by spending time with them, inviting them to meals and trying to get to know them. This should not be done artificially but sincerely because we are really interested in them for the sake of their own eternal welfare.

Dear Christian reader, we have all been called to be faithful 'stewards of the mysteries of God' and of 'the faith which was once for all delivered to the saints'. May we be found faithful to God who has appointed us to this task, faithful to the *message* he has committed to our trust, and faithful to his *people* who are looking to us for spiritual nutrition. 'I feel there are two things it is impossible to desire with sufficient ardour', said Robert Murray M'Cheyne, 'personal holiness and the honour of Christ in the salvation of souls.'

KEY THOUGHTS

KEY THOUGHTS

There can be no Christian stewardship without guarding from error the Word of truth God has entrusted to us in the Bible and faithfully passing it on to others. This is the only way for anyone to come to know Jesus Christ and to grow more and more in his likeness. Without the Christian message we have nothing of eternal worth to give to others.

Our faithful stewardship of all the other God-given resources we have considered so far will accomplish nothing — for God's honour or the eternal well-being of our fellow men and women — if they are not used for promoting the gospel. If God's glory is to be the end, God's Word must be the means.

QUESTIONS FOR DISCUSSION

1. What is Jude 3 referring to when it speaks of 'the faith which was once for all delivered to the saints', and what is our responsibility to it? Give biblical references to support your answers.

2. Who does the New Testament say are stewards of the faith or the mysteries of God? Again, give at least two proof-texts.

3. Why does Paul say in Romans 1:14, 'I am a debtor both to Greeks and to barbarians'? Does it apply to all Christians?

4. Read Luke 16:9–10,19–31; 1 Corinthians 1:18–25; 2:1–5; 3:1–4; Hebrews 5:11–14 and 2 Timothy 3:15 and enumerate what faithfulness in stewardship of God's Word will mean for its Christian and non-Christian hearers.

SUGGESTIONS FOR PRAYER

1. Thank God for revealing and preserving his truth in the written words of Holy Scripture and for using it by the Spirit's power

PRAYER

to bring you to faith in Jesus Christ.

2. *Pray for more grace from the Holy Spirit to love the truth and to study and understand it so that you may be approved by God as 'a worker who does not need to be ashamed, rightly dividing the word of truth' (2 Tim. 2:15).*

3. *Ask God to help you to be built up in your faith, to use you to strengthen other Christians and to use your witness to save sinners by 'pulling them out of the fire' (Jude 23).*

Ah, when I look up at that Cross,
Where God's great Steward suffered loss —
Yea, loss of life and blood for me!
A trifling thing it seems to be
To pay the tithe, dear Lord, to Thee
Of time, or talent, wealth or store —
Full well I know I owe Thee more;
A million times I owe Thee more.

But that is just the reason why
I lift my heart to God on high
And pledge Thee by this portion small
My life, my love, my all in all!
This holy token at Thy Cross
I know, as gold, must seem but dross,
But in my heart, Lord, Thou dost see
How it has pledged my all to Thee,
That I steward true may be!

— *Bishop Ralph S. Cushman (1879–1960)*

CHAPTER EIGHT

THE STEWARDSHIP OF OUR MONEY

LOOK IT UP

Honour the Lord with your possessions,
And with the firstfruits of all your increase (Prov. 3:9).

He who sows sparingly will also reap sparingly,
and he who sows bountifully will also reap bountifully.
So let each one give as he purposes in his heart,
not grudgingly or of necessity; for God loves
a cheerful giver. And God is able to make all grace
abound toward you, that you, always having
all sufficiency in all things, may have an abundance
for every good work (2 Cor. 9:6–8).

INTRODUCTION

Money is the most difficult asset to manage for the glory of God and the good of others because it is the thing we loved most before our conversion and the thing that offers most resistance to faithful Christian stewardship after conversion. Our wallet and our cheque-book are usually the last things to be fully surrendered to Christ. It is commonly said that 'money is the root of all evil', but like many other everyday sayings that have been taken from the Bible, it has not been quoted correctly. What Paul actually said was, 'The love of money is a root of all kinds of evil' (1 Tim. 6:10). For money itself is amoral; it is neither good nor bad. It is our *attitude* to money that is either right or wrong.

In this sense it is quite correct to say that money talks. For whether or not we want to talk about money, money talks about us. One way to judge our character is to discover how we earn and spend our money. Do we earn it honestly? Do we spend it wisely and charitably?

But money also talks about our souls. A good way to gauge our love for Christ is to consider if our giving to Christ is sacrificial. True, we can give without loving Jesus, but we cannot love Jesus without giving to him. We love that to which we give, and we give to that which we love. So, then, it is important to talk about the stewardship of our money. In this chapter I want to be very practical and consider questions like the following: Who is to give to God's work? What are they to give? When should they give? And to whom should they give? These are important questions and only in understanding the answers that follow can we hope to be responsible stewards of our money.

Giving is the duty of all Christians

Scripture declares that giving is the duty of all Christians. This is clearly taught in 1 Corinthians 16:2: 'Let each one of you lay something aside.' And again in 2 Corinthians 9:7: 'So let each one give as he purposes in his heart.' Paul was taking up a collection for the struggling Christians in Judea and his command to give is directed to 'each one'. Even though it was a special offering there were to be no exceptions in the church.

EXPLANATION

It is amazing how easily we can persuade ourselves that we cannot give at the moment. If we are enrolled in school or university we say, 'My pocket money or allowance is too small. No one can expect me to give.' Singles can argue: 'I just have one income to manage a home and a car and everything else. No one can expect me to give.' The courting couple can argue: 'We have our bottom drawer to fill. We're saving to get married. No one can expect us to give.' Newly-weds or young parents can argue: 'We are buying furniture and paying off our home. No one can expect us to give.' The middle-aged couple can say, 'Our children are at a very expensive stage. We need all we have to finish their education and help set them up in life. No one can expect us to give.' The retired couple can argue: 'We are living on a pension and we have high medical expenses. No one can expect old-age pensioners to give.'

So, by the time we have allowed for all of these periods of small pay or big expenses, there is never a good time in life for us to give. This is unacceptable as far as God is concerned. Christians should begin to realize that every time of life is a time for giving to the Lord's work. Let the schoolboy begin with his allowance and carry on right through to his old-age pension.

Then, too, we are all expected to give *whatever our means*. Let us not make the mistake of leaving the privilege of giving to those members of the

church whom we imagine to be better off. This attitude
is wrong for two reasons. First, we should give to show
our *gratitude* to the Lord for his many mercies to us
(Prov. 3:9). Some of us are poorer than others, granted.
But the poorest of us has cause to thank the Lord for our
salvation, for we 'know the grace of our Lord Jesus
Christ, that though he was rich, yet for [our] sakes he
became poor, that [we] through his poverty might
become rich' (2 Cor. 8:9). We should say thank you with
our tangible gifts, no matter how small they may be.
The day to stop giving to the Lord is the day when we
have nothing to say thank you for.

Second, our poverty has nothing to do with the value
of our giving in God's sight. The value of each gift to
God is judged by the *means* of the giver. As has often
been said, God does not look at what we give but at
what is left over. That is the lesson of the familiar story
of the widow and her two mites. The poor woman
could not hope to compete with the rich Pharisees who
conscientiously tithed their large incomes and she
never imagined that anyone would take note of the
tiny offering that she deposited in the collection box in
the temple. But Jesus had seen her and he esteemed her
gift as the biggest of the day, saying, 'Truly, I say to you,
that this poor widow has put in more than all; for all
these out of their abundance have put in offerings for
God, but she out of her poverty put in all the livelihood
that she had' (Luke 21:3–4)

Now because few of us are as poor as this widow
we may (and we must) all fulfil our duty in Christian
giving. Indeed, like this widow the poorest of us can be

the biggest givers in God's sight for our gifts are measured in heaven not by their *size* but by their *sacrifice*.

We should give proportionately to our means

Scripture reveals to us that we should give proportionately to our means. In order that the responsibility of supporting God's work may be equitably distributed among his people, the Old Testament laid down a basic formula for giving: each one was to give at least one-tenth of their total income to God for the support of the tribe of Levi, as the Levites were set apart to the service of God (Num. 18:21–32). No one was to give less than a tenth, and even the Levites who received the tithe had to give a tenth of that to the high priest. But if the tithe is a *floor* from which we are to start giving, it is certainly not meant to be a *ceiling* at which we stop giving. Rather it is the privilege of all God's people to give him as much as they can above one-tenth.

Before the biblical grounds for this view are laid out it is important to acknowledge that there is another view of Christian giving that is much more widely held than the one just suggested. It is the view that the New Testament teaches that Christians should give as God enables them. The more he prospers them the more they should give.

Tithing, it is claimed, is legalistic or can easily degenerate into legalism when it becomes a duty imposed on us, rather than something we delight to do. Tithing, it is thought, limits Christian giving to one-tenth per person. It is also argued that the poor are unable to tithe because their meagre earnings are barely enough to survive on. So it is sincerely believed that the New Testament does not endorse tithing as a minimum percentage for every Christian to give. Instead, they say, Paul instructs the Christians in Galatia and Greece to take up a collection for their fellow believers in Judea and commands each one to 'lay something aside, storing up as he may prosper' (1 Cor. 16:2). And again, regarding the same collection, he directs that 'each one give as he purposes in his heart, not grudgingly or of necessity; for God loves a cheerful giver' (2 Cor. 9:7).

Now if these two references are the main guidelines in the New Testament for all Christian giving, then giving as God enables us and giving generously as we purpose in our hearts is clearly the New Testament principle for determining what a believer should give to God's work. But do these references cover all Christian giving, or are they applicable only to giving to special causes outside the local church's ministry? That is the crucial question. So let us consider how the principle of proportionate giving is enunciated in both the Old and the New Testaments.

1. The Old Testament
The Jewish people were commanded by God in Leviticus to give a tithe to the Lord that was one-tenth of their total

EXPLANATION

income. This is what the law of God said, 'All
the tithe of the land, whether of the seed of the
land or of the fruit of the tree, is the Lord's. It is
holy to the Lord... And concerning the tithe of
the herd of the flock, ... the tenth one shall be
holy to the Lord' (Lev. 27:30,32). Thus one-tenth
of the produce of the ground and one-tenth of
the increase of their livestock belonged to God.
It was to be given to him for the support of the
Levites who served in his house of worship
(Num. 18:21,24).

Then again, three times each year — at the
Feast of Passover, the Feast of Weeks and the Feast
of Tabernacles — the Jews had to bring thank
offerings to God over and above their tithe. Moses
is told, 'They shall not appear before the Lord
empty-handed. Every man shall give as he is able,
according to the blessing of the Lord your God
which he has given you' (Deut. 16:16–17). And
then on top of this, their firstfruits at harvest, the
firstborn of their animals, their sin offerings and
peace offerings, and so on, were all to be given in
addition to the tithe.

But that was not all. When the time came to
build the tabernacle, God said to Moses, 'Speak
to the children of Israel, that they bring me an
offering. From everyone who gives it willingly
with his heart you shall take my offering' (Exod.
25:2). The people brought freewill offerings to
the Lord of every valuable thing. Indeed so great
was the response that Moses had to restrain them

from bringing anything more. 'Then everyone came whose heart was stirred, and everyone whose spirit was willing, and they brought the Lord's offering for the work of the tabernacle of meeting... Then all the craftsmen... spoke to Moses, saying, "The people bring much more than enough for the service of the work which the Lord commanded us to do"' (Exod. 35:21; 36:4–5). Later, when the temple was to be built, David made a similar appeal to the people of Israel. The cost of this expensive project was to come not from the tithe which was for the support of the Levites, but from freewill offerings (1 Chr. 29:6–9).

So the principle of giving in the Old Testament is very plain. Every Israelite who earned an income had to give one-tenth of it to the Levites for their services and they in turn had to give a tithe of what they received to the priests (Num. 18:25–28). Over and above this, every Israelite had to give regular thank offerings as well, but no set amount was laid down for these additional gifts. Each man had to give as he was able and according to the measure in which God had blessed him. Even in the choosing of a sin offering he could choose according to his means. If he could not afford a lamb or a goat he could offer a pair of turtle doves as a sacrifice to God instead. And then there were the freewill offerings given for special needs like the building of the sanctuary of God or given out of the worshipper's gratitude for some particular blessing bestowed by God. Now as we turn to the teaching of the New Testament, we will see that the same principle of giving by the people of God is enunciated there.

EXPLANATION

2. The New Testament

First of all, like the Old Testament, the New Testament insists that the primary responsibility of the people of God is to support those who are set apart to the service of God (Matt. 10:7–10; Rom. 10:15). Paul therefore says in 1 Corinthians 9:14, 'Even so the Lord has commanded that those who preach the gospel should live from the gospel.' And again he says, 'Let him who is taught the word share all good things with him who teaches' (Gal. 6:6). That is God's clear command. Just as the Jews had to support the priests and Levites who worked in the temple, so Christians must support pastors and missionaries who serve in the church (God's new temple). In 1 Corinthians 9:1–14 Paul refers to many Old Testament laws to support the continuance of this principle of giving in the New Testament.

But that is not the end of a Christian's responsibility to give. Like the Jews, believers today should give special offerings over and above their regular contribution to their local church. Thus when Paul sought to raise funds to help the believers in Jerusalem he did not ask the churches to make a donation from their general funds. Instead, he organized a separate collection. And he instructs the Christians in the churches of Greece and Galatia to set aside a separate offering each week for those impoverished Christians (1 Cor. 16:1). Although he commands every Christian to contribute to this collection, he does not specify a fixed proportion or amount for them to bring. He says in 2 Corinthians 9:7, 'So let each one give as he purposes in his heart, not grudgingly or of necessity; for God loves a cheerful giver.' So the principle of giving in both Testaments is the same in that over and above our regular contribution to his work God expects us to give separate offerings to other good causes for advancing his kingdom.

Now it is true that the New Testament contains no direct command to Christians to tithe to the church, but there are two good reasons why Christians should consider tithing as the starting point of their giving to God. First, tithing did not originate at Mount Sinai, and so it is not part of the ceremonial law of the Old Testament, which Christ through the cross has set aside (Matt. 15:20; Gal.4:9–10; Col. 2:16–17; Heb. 10:1–10). The tithing principle was actually evident a long time prior to Moses. Thus we read back in Genesis that Abraham 'gave a tithe of all' to Melchizedek 'the priest of God Most High' (Gen. 14:18–20) whom the writer of Hebrews describes as 'without father, without mother, without genealogy, having neither beginning of days nor end of life, but made like the Son of God' (Heb. 7:1–10). If Melchizedek, then, is a pre-incarnate appearance of the Son of God, should not we like Abraham, 'who is the father of us all' (Rom. 4:16), give our tithe to Christ as well? If it is objected that Melchizedek was not a pre-incarnate appearance of Christ it can still be argued that because Abraham offered tithes to Melchizedek as he exercised his priestly office for God Most High, then we should not do less as we give our offerings to Christ who is

EXPLANATION

'High Priest forever according to the order of Melchizedek' (Heb. 6:20). There can be no dispute, however, that Jacob gave a tenth of all his income to Christ (Gen. 28:20–22). For the Lord who appeared to Jacob on this occasion was Jehovah, and the New Testament writers equate Jehovah with Jesus Christ. To take only one example, in Isaiah 45:23 Jehovah says, 'To me every knee shall bow, every tongue shall take an oath'; then in Romans 14:9–11 and Philippians 2:10–11 Paul applies these very words to Jesus Christ.

Second, Christians should give a minimum of one-tenth of our income to Christ and his church because we enjoy far greater blessings under his grace than the Jews ever had under the law, and therefore we would not want the Jews to exceed us in giving to God's work. If Jews were compelled by law to give a tenth to God, how can we, constrained by love, give less? The sad fact of the matter is that many Christians are giving much less than one-tenth of their income to God. According to a report in *Christianity Today* the per capita giving of church members in America in 1995 was a mere 2.55 per cent. Although these statistics no doubt include a proportion of unregenerate professing Christians, they are nevertheless disturbing.

Now someone may say, 'You know, I would like to tithe my income, but I honestly do not think I can afford to do so.' How are we to respond to that? Simply this, giving is not a matter of generosity but of honesty. All that we have belongs to God and not to us (1 Cor. 6:19–20). So to withhold your tithe (which is a token and acknowledgement of this fact) is not just unfaithful stewardship, it is to 'rob God' and incur his displeasure (Mal. 3:8–9).

Conversely, when we give at least a tithe of our income to God's house, his promise through Malachi is that he will 'open for you the windows of heaven and pour out for you such blessing that there will not be room enough to receive it' (Mal. 3:10). The blessings may or may not be financial ones. In all probability they will be spiritual blessings and we should not deprive ourselves of these by disobeying God's command to tithe. Our income may be below the poverty level but throughout the ages God has wonderfully provided for poor believers. David says in Psalm 37:25–26,

I have been young, and now am old;
Yet I have not seen the righteous forsaken,
Nor his descendents begging bread.
He is ever merciful, and lends;
And his descendants are blessed.

God knows how to make a little go a long way as Elijah and the widow in Zarephath proved (1 Kings 17:8–16).

God is no man's debtor. He is jealous of his reputation as a bountiful giver. Indeed, how could any believer ever outdo God! So Paul says we must not give 'reluctantly or under compulsion, for God loves a cheerful giver. And God is able to provide you with every blessing in abundance, so that you may always have enough of everything and may provide in abundance for every good work' (2 Cor. 9:8, RSV).

Jesus made a similar promise: 'Give, and it will be given you: good measure, pressed down, shaken together, and running over will be put into your bosom. For with the same measure that you use, it will be measured back to you' (Luke 6:38). These (and there are others) are great promises. What they simply mean is that no one, whether they have little or much, will be the poorer for giving to God. If times are hard and we must tighten our belts, let us not economize on our giving. That is false economy because to stint in our giving to the Lord's house, says the prophet Haggai, is to 'earn wages to put into a bag with holes' (Hag. 1:6).

THINK ABOUT IT

A giving Saviour should have giving disciples.
— *J. C. Ryle*

Shall we grudge the expenses of our religion, or starve so good a cause?
— *Matthew Henry*

Whatever we part with for God's sake shall be made up to us in kind or kindness.
— *Matthew Henry*

If God gave you ten times as much as you give him, could
you live on it?
— *Anonymous*

It could be argued that in the Old Testament tithes were
paid, and therefore do not, strictly speaking, come under
the heading of giving at all. Christian giving only begins
when we give more than a tenth.'
— *Kenneth F. W. Prior*

Giving should be
performed systematically

We should be methodical not only in *what we give* but
when we give. The apostle Paul says in 1 Corinthians
16:1–2 that we must bring even our special offerings to
church on the Lord's day. Paul planned to get to Corinth
in about a year's time, but he still commands the
Corinthians to bring something each week for the relief
fund so that their gifts would be ready to be taken to
Jerusalem when he arrived.

To be haphazard in our giving, giving as the whim
takes us or giving what happens to be in our pocket
when we are in church and giving nothing when we
are absent, is not God's way. Our giving to the Lord's
work through his church must be done as regularly
and punctually as the paying of our personal bills
and accounts.

One thing is certain. If we do not give priority to our
Christian giving we will find it crowded out by other

financial commitments, and the Lord's work will suffer. We must avoid the weakness of the farmer whose best cow gave birth to twin calves: one brown and the other white. In his excitement he ran indoors to tell his wife the good news and announce that he had decided in gratitude to give one calf to the Lord. Both calves would be brought up together, he said, then one would be sold and the proceeds given to the church. His more matter-of-fact wife, however, asked him which of the two calves he intended to dedicate to the Lord. 'Ah', he said, 'there's no need to decide that now. We can do it later.' A few months passed, and then one day the farmer came into the kitchen looking very miserable. 'My dear', he sighed, 'I have bad news. The Lord's calf is dead.' 'The Lord's calf?' exclaimed his wife in astonishment. 'But I thought you said you hadn't decided which calf would be the Lord's.' 'Yes', he said, 'but I always thought it would be the white one.'

The Lord's calf has a way of dying, does it not? One of the greatest difficulties in Christian giving is to keep the Lord's calf alive. That is the value of using church offering envelopes for our giving. It is so easy to go away on vacation or to be off sick and to forget our weekly or monthly contribution. But dated, anonymous envelopes can assist us in keeping our giving regular and systematic.

Giving is a duty to be
performed purposefully

We have seen from Scripture that we are to support God's servants, the building and maintenance of his sanctuary, the advancement of his kingdom and the poor, especially those of the household of faith (Acts 11:27–30; Gal. 2:10; 6:10). These needs are of vital concern for the glory of God and the doing of his will. God gave clear instructions in the Old Testament for the tithe to be brought to his house. In 2 Chronicles 31:11 we read, 'Hezekiah commanded them to prepare rooms in the house of the Lord... Then they faithfully brought in... the tithes.' In Malachi 3:10 we have the command, 'Bring all the tithes into the storehouse, that there may be food in my house' (cf. Amos 4:4). The tithe belonged to God. No Jew had the right to decide where or how it ought to be spent. The 'whole tithe' (Mal. 3:10, NASB) had to go to God's house.

I want to suggest that the same principle must apply in the New Testament for at least two reasons. First, God's church (made up of many local churches) has replaced God's temple in Jerusalem (Matt. 16:13–19; John 4:21–24; 2 Cor. 6:16; Eph. 2:19–22) as the only body that is essential for the worship of God and the witness of his Word. God's work can still go forward without Bible societies, parachurch groups or radio or television stations but God's work cannot be done without well-supported local churches. That is the crux of the matter. Therefore the local church must never suffer a lack of support because of parachurch work. As vital and necessary as some of these other organizations are, they are no substitute for the local church. Prior claim for our support must go to the church that Christ is building (1 Cor. 9:1–14; 1 Tim. 5:17–18). It is the only essential and eternal society in the purposes of God.

Second, the tithe must go to the local church where we worship because its support cannot be left to the discretion of its members. This is the very reason why many local churches are under-supported. Many members just give what they fancy, and some give nothing at all because they feel that their money is needed elsewhere. But our giving to the local church cannot be governed by what we feel or what we think. Certainly the government could not run our country if our taxes were based on such a system. How then can Christians think that God's church can operate on such inefficient lines? No, God would not leave so vital a matter to personal feeling. The Bible and common sense demand that each member must accept their rightful share of this responsibility, and the pattern provided for us in the Old Testament is that it should be a minimum of ten per cent of our total income.

However, the argument does not stop there. Tithing to our local church is not only *equitable*, it is also *ethical*. Why should some Christians enjoy the blessing of a paid ministry and expensive buildings without accepting their rightful share of the costs? What would you think of a citizen who evaded paying taxes but enjoyed the benefits that other citizens were paying for? You would call it dishonest. Well, by the same token it is unethical to evade tithing to the local church.

But, some argue, what about the support of Christian work outside of the local church? Who is going to support that work? We must. But parachurch work must be supported not by tithes but by freewill offerings of God's people. And this is where generosity and sacrifice come into the picture. I am not being generous when I tithe to the church. I am simply giving to God what is rightfully his. It belongs to him. Generosity only begins with what I give out of the remaining nine-tenths, and Christians should be the most generous of all people. No one has received more of the grace of God's salvation or more of the knowledge of his truth than Christians.

The churches at Macedonia were poor and persecuted, but they were wonderfully generous in their support of Paul's fund for the Jerusalem church and so he used them as an example to spur on the tardy but richer Corinthians. The apostle writes,

> Now, brethren, we wish to make known to you the grace of God which has been given in the churches of Macedonia, that in a great ordeal of affliction their abundance of joy and their deep poverty overflowed in the wealth of their liberality. For I testify that according to their ability, and beyond their ability, they gave of their own accord, begging us with much urging for the favor of participation

in the support of the saints (2 Cor. 8:1–4, NASB).

'Going beyond the call of duty' is a phrase used of military bravery, and it is in going beyond the range of personal ability that the real splendour of Christian giving lies. Let us never insult the Lord of glory by offering to him that which involves no sacrifice. David, conscious of this danger, made this resolve: 'I will not offer burnt offerings to the Lord my God which cost me nothing' (2 Sam. 24:24, RSV).

Perhaps the greatest hindrance to generosity in Christian giving is the natural and selfish tendency to neutralize every increase in our income with a corresponding increase in our standard of living. A Gallup poll taken in October 1988 showed that the more money Americans made, the less sacrificial their giving became. Those making less than $10,000 per annum gave an average of 2.8 per cent of their income each year to churches and charities. Those making $10,000 to $30,000 gave an average of 2.5 per cent; those making $30,000 to $50,000 gave 2 per cent; and those making $50,000 to $75,000 gave a total of only 1.5 per cent to their church and other non-profit organizations. Giving is not sacrificial unless it is a sacrifice. If we are making more money this year than we did last year but giving the same percentage of our income that we were giving before, then we are not giving sacrificially. We may be giving a larger amount than we gave before but actually sacrificing less financially for the kingdom of God. The reason for the deficiency of Christian giving today lies not with the inability of the poor but with the selfishness of the rich (1 Tim. 6:17–19). How vital it is that Christians in the affluent West heed the words of our Master in the parable of the unfaithful steward: 'For everyone to whom much is given, from him much will be required; and to whom much has been committed, of him they will ask the more' (Luke 12:48).

How different it was with the selfless John Wesley who from the sale of his books alone gave away between £30,000 to £40,000. When he died his personal estate amounted to only a few pounds. What was the secret of his sustained generosity? Simply this, he kept a close check on his standard of living. When he was an Oxford undergraduate and still unconverted, his income for the first year was £30 while his frugal expenses were £26. The remaining £4 he gave to the Lord's work. The next year his income doubled. Did he double his giving? Yes, nine times over. He said, 'I lived comfortably on £26 last year, I can do so again.' So instead of raising his standard of living he gave the whole of his increase in salary (£34) to God. The next year his income was £90 and he gave away £64.

John Wesley increased his standard of living only when it was necessary. Little wonder that God entrusted him with so much. One of the last entries in his diary reads as follows: 'From upwards of eighty-six years I have kept my accounts exactly. I will not attempt it any longer, being satisfied with the continual conviction that I must save all I can and give all I can.' His is an example worthy of emulation.

The fact that we are called to remain on the home front does not mean that we should enjoy a higher standard of living than the missionary on a foreign field. If we need a suitable home, good clothes, money to educate our children and a livable pension, should not God's servants at home and abroad have the same? The sacrifices made for the sake of the gospel, says Paul, should be equal (2 Cor. 8:13–15, NEB). There is no double standard of living in the New Testament — one for those in secular employment and another for so-called full time Christian workers. The purpose of Christian giving, says Paul, is not to bring 'ease' to those who receive the gift by bringing 'hardship' to those who give 'but that there may be equality'.

Once again this is not only a New Testament standard for Paul illustrates his point from Exodus 16:18 where it refers to the gathering of manna in the wilderness. When the manna came down from heaven early each morning, the Israelites were to collect just what they needed for that day. Hoarding was not permitted. Those who gathered too much could not keep it because it turned bad overnight. On the other hand those who gathered too little never lacked for they received from those who had collected too much. There was equality. The one's abundance supplied the other's lack. And that is how it should be among

Christians too. Our abundance should supply the lack of those in need, and, when things change, their abundance should supply our lack so 'that there may be equality' (2 Cor. 8:14).

So we come to the question: How are we to practice these principles? Paul provides the answer in 2 Corinthians 8. In verse 7 he says, 'But as you abound in everything — in faith, in speech, in knowledge, in all diligence, and in your love for us — see that you abound [or excel] in this grace also.' That is to say, in the grace of generous giving that the Macedonian churches abounded in. But how? The answer is found first in verse 1 where God's grace is said to have been 'bestowed on' or given to the Macedonians and then in verse 9 where God's grace is said to be known in Christ who was 'rich, yet for your sakes he became poor, that you through his poverty might become rich'.

Grace is the key. It is God's grace *displayed* in the self-emptying of Christ's birth and death that inspires and challenges us to give, whereas it is God's grace *bestowed* on us through the Holy Spirit that enables us to overflow in liberal giving to others. The more we contemplate God's grace in Christ and the more we pray for God's grace in our hearts, the more generously we will give to extend the cause of Christ's kingdom. Christian giving is grace giving. It is compelled by love and not by law, love that wants to keep God's commandments because that is what pleases him (John 14:21), and love that is grateful to God for his immeasurable sacrifice for sinners on Calvary. Giving that is not compelled by such love will never please God.

This is true of all relationships. If you bring home a gold necklace for your wife on the anniversary of your wedding, she will probably say, 'Oh, sweetheart, it's exquisite! Thank you so much! But why did you buy me such an expensive gift?' If, however, you were to respond by saying, 'My dear, don't you know that it's a husband's duty to give his wife a gift on their anniversary?' how do you think she would feel? She would probably wish that you had not bothered to buy her anything at all. And who would blame her? But if you replied, 'My darling, I did it because I wanted to show you how much I love you', she would be overjoyed. Why? Because the former act would have been motivated by a sense of duty but the latter by sheer love — and that makes all the difference in the world. Does God have less feeling than we do? Of course not! He wants our giving to be inspired by our love for him and not by a sense of duty.

Before I conclude this aspect of stewardship I must say something about what Dr A. J. Gordon called 'extra-corpus benevolence'. Our adversary, Satan, has many devices for drying up the spring of generosity in a Christian's soul, and thus preventing the giving of funds for spreading God's Word. One of his tricks is to persuade believers to postpone their liberality until after their death, by leaving a substantial amount to Christian causes in their wills. Oh, you can give regular token amounts while you are alive, but leave the big amount for when you leave this world. In his disarming way Dr Gordon makes it clear that we will receive God's reward for the personal sacrifices we made in this life — for 'the things done in the body... whether good or bad' (2 Cor. 5:10).

It is, of course, a wise and good thing to include God's work in our wills. But there is surely no sacrifice involved when what is given, is given when it is no longer of any use to us. We would do well again to remember David's response to Araunah the Jebusite when he offered to give the king the oxen needed to offer a burnt sacrifice to God. David declined saying, 'No, but I will surely buy it from you for a price; nor will I offer burnt offerings to the Lord my God with that which costs me nothing' (2 Sam. 24:24).

The reverse side of this device of Satan is to trick us into not making any provision at all in our wills for the Lord's work. It is wrong to say that the money has already been tithed so there is no further need to give to world evangelization; we have done our duty. But is it wise to leave all our money to heirs who may well have enough of their own or may use it in a way that will not glorify God? Trenchant are the words:

What I spend, I lose;
What I keep will be left to others;
What I give away will remain forever mine.

It is time for many of us to stop tipping the Almighty God. He wants and deserves our unsparing gifts not our patronizing gratuities. Christians are failing more in their stewardship of money than in any other area. According to a study in 2000 by the well-reputed Barna Research Group in America, sixty-six per cent of all adults made a gift to a church in 1998; two years later only sixty-one per cent gave. The average donation fell from $806 to $649. That same year thirty-two per cent of people who classified themselves as born-again Christians said they tithed. But when a comparison was made between their household income and their gifts, only twelve per cent actually tithed either their net or gross incomes (even though many Christians in America today speak of their giving as tithing). These statistics impress on us the serious need for more faithful teaching today on the stewardship of money.

KEY THOUGHTS

Wonderful things could be done in evangelizing the world if every Christian would accept these four basic principles of Christian giving. *One*, giving is a responsibility to be performed by all Christians, whatever our age and whatever our means. *Two*, giving is a responsibility to be performed proportionately to our means, remembering that one-tenth of our income is the minimum amount that God requires from his people. *Three*, giving is a responsibility to be performed systematically in sickness and in health, at home or on vacation, whenever we receive our pay. *Four*, giving is a responsibility to be performed purposefully, taking care first to give the Lord's tithe to our local church and then assisting other Christian causes as we are able from the remaining nine-tenths. Let us adopt these principles immediately, for by them God will be honoured, Christ's church will be blessed and the gospel will be preached to every nation.

QUESTIONS FOR DISCUSSION

1. *Summarize the principles of giving enunciated in both the Old and New Testaments as indicated in the following verses: Exodus 25:1–9; Leviticus 27:30,32; Numbers 18:21–32; Deuteronomy 16:16–17; 1 Chronicles 29:6–9; Matthew 10:7–10; Romans 10:15; 1 Corinthians 9:1–14; 1 Corinthians 16:1–4; Galatians 6:6.*

2. *Discuss the merits of the following statement: A tithe to a rich person (and most Christians in the West are rich compared with most Christians in the Third World) is no sacrifice at all, but a poor man's tithe is already a very real sacrifice. Use Paul's teaching in 2 Corinthians 8 and 9 as a frame of reference.*

3. *If tithing (unlike circumcision) predates Abraham (for Abraham was not commanded to tithe his income — it was already an existing practice), and if tithing (unlike circumcision) is not specifically revoked and replaced by something else in the New Testament, do you think it can be justifiably claimed that tithing is as timeless a principle as the*

DISCUSS IT

Sabbath, and that just as God claims one-seventh of his people's time, so he claims one-tenth of their income? Refer to Genesis 14:18–20; 17:9–14; Matthew 23:23; Luke 11:42; Acts 15:3–21; Galatians 2:3; 5:6; 6:15; and Colossians 2:11–12 before you formulate your answer.

4. If someone is convinced that a Christian should tithe their income, do you think it should be based on gross income or net income (on what remains after pension, medical and other benefits have been deducted)? Give the reasons for your answer.

5. Why do you think the question of whether or not a Christian should tithe to his or her local church is not addressed in the New Testament?
   a. Is it because everyone assumed that tithing was no longer relevant because each Christian had to make up their own mind on the issue?
   b. Is it because tithing was so obvious a responsibility to the many Jewish Christians in the church that questioning its continued practice was unthinkable?
   c. Do you have another reason?

SUGGESTIONS FOR PRAYER

1. Give praise to God as the giver of every good and perfect gift and thank him for all your material blessings.

2. *If you have failed to properly honour God with your substance, ask for his forgiveness.*

3. *Pray that God's grace displayed at Calvary may be abundantly bestowed on you through the Holy Spirit to enable you to give sacrificially to God's work and to resist any temptation to unnecessarily increase your standard of living.*

In a land far away stood a home Jesus loved
    And He often to it would repair,
'Twas where Mary and Martha and Lazarus lived
    And a welcome awaited Him there.

In that old-fashioned home God was ever supreme,
    And their faith was as bright as the sun,
And their sorrow and death were soon turned into joy,
    By their guest, the victorious One.

Oh that old-fashioned home to which Jesus would come,
    It was dearer than all else beside;
And I'm praying each day, just to live Jesus' way
    That my Lord in my home may abide.

— *Chauncey R. Piety (b.1885)*

CHAPTER NINE

THE STEWARDSHIP OF OUR HOME

LOOK IT UP

⟨BIBLE REFERENCE⟩

Let love be without hypocrisy…
Be kindly affectionate to one another with brotherly
love, in honour giving preference to one another…
distributing to the needs of the saints,
given to hospitality
(Rom. 12:9–10,13).

INTRODUCTION

The home is another neglected area of Christian stewardship. I would venture to say that in the average church most members have not been in each other's homes. And yet hospitality is a Christian virtue; it is an expression of our faith. For Paul it was such an important expression of Christian faith that he lists it among the qualifications of a church elder or bishop (the words are used interchangeably in the New Testament). In 1 Timothy 3:2 he says that a bishop must be hospitable, and in Titus 1:7–8 he says that 'a bishop must be blameless, as a steward of God, … hospitable, a lover of what is good'. In other words he is not just to visit other people in their homes, he is to invite them to his own home for fellowship and food.

But the grace of hospitality is by no means to be confined to those who hold the office of an elder or a pastor. The willingness to provide hospitality, says Paul, is also the test of a Christian woman's character. He writes to Timothy: 'Honour widows who are widows indeed; having a reputation for good works; and if she has brought up children, if she has shown hospitality to strangers, if she has washed the saints' feet' (1 Tim. 5:3,10, NASB). Peter, in turn, exhorts all Christians: 'Be hospitable to one another without grumbling' (1 Peter 4:9). And in Hebrews 13:2 the author says, 'Do not forget to entertain strangers.'

Paul also includes hospitality in his list of virtues in Romans 12 as he explains what it means to present our bodies as 'a living sacrifice' to God. He writes, 'Be kindly affectionate to one another with brotherly love... distributing to the needs of the saints, given to hospitality' (Rom. 12:10,13).

Indeed, it is significant to note that the early church practised hospitality extensively. Luke records that after Pentecost they broke bread 'from house to house' (Acts 2:46). Moreover, in the early church the Lord's Supper was always preceded by a communal meal in which the food that each family brought was shared (1 Cor. 11:17–22,33). Now I appreciate that some people do not have a home to use. You may live with your parents, in a college dormitory or in an army barrack. If so, remember that our Lord did not have a home either. He said, 'Foxes have holes and the birds of the air have nests, but the Son of Man has nowhere to lay his head' (Matt. 8:20). So to offer hospitality was something Jesus could not do. But what he did do was to accept hospitality graciously, and we will have something to say near the end of this chapter about being a gracious guest. However the day will come when you are in a position to give hospitality, and you will then discover that it is indeed 'more blessed to give than to receive', as our Lord said (Acts 20:35).

What is Christian hospitality?

EXPLANATION

The *Oxford Dictionary* describes hospitality as 'friendly and liberal reception of guests or strangers'. Christian hospitality, then, is to do this in the name of Christ and for his sake. Having said that, it needs to be pointed out that Christian hospitality is not simply a matter of catering. Some people just love entertaining visitors and organizing get-togethers for adults and children. Others find it a strain. They spend ages getting the food ready and everything looking right, and when it is all over they heave a sigh of relief.

But Christian hospitality is more than that. It is the giving of time and help to our brothers and sisters in need. It may be in the form of a bed for a night or two, having a family over for a meal when the mother is in hospital or just a sympathetic ear to a burdened soul over a cup of coffee. You may not have the facilities or the means to provide a seven-course meal, but you can offer them something to eat and drink in the name of Christ. Hospitality can be quite simple.

This was something that Martha of Bethany found hard to understand. Martha and Mary were both noble women and friends of Jesus. They were both hospitable, but Martha overdid it. She thought that hospitality consisted in serving a really good meal. Of course, there are times and occasions when we should do that, and it would be wonderful if more of us did it more often. But Christian hospitality is more than just catering or entertaining. When Jesus came to the home of Mary and Martha that day, the thing he wanted most of all was Christian fellowship (Luke 10:38-42).

Our Lord was probably tired, hungry and thirsty after his travels that day but greater than his physical need was his desire to share with others the things of God. Mary understood this and while her sister Martha was busy in the kitchen, Mary 'sat at Jesus' feet and heard his word'. Martha, however, as Luke records:

> ... was distracted with much serving, and she approached him and said, 'Lord, do you not care that my sister has left me to serve alone? Therefore tell her to help me.' And Jesus answered and said to her, 'Martha, Martha, you are worried and troubled about many things [the many things she was preparing]. But one thing is needed, and Mary has chosen that good part, which will not be taken away from her.'

Our Lord is clearly saying that a scrumptious meal is not his top priority. We all need food for the body, but we need something infinitely more important than that. We need food for our souls. Mary had chosen the better part of God's blessing and Jesus would not deprive her of the spiritual food he could give her.

EXPLANATION

'Given to hospitality' does not mean elaborate catering. It means a home where someone who wants to talk something out or pray something through can just drop in and do so. It means having a home that is open all the time to help and encourage those who need your friendship and fellowship (whether it is over a cup of tea or a meal). To practise such hospitality will mean the use of some time and energy, some cost to our finances and the loss of a little privacy. But it is a wonderful service to Christ and his church.

The blessing of Christian hospitality

Christianity was never meant to be confined, as it so often is, to public buildings and to Sundays. During the week our homes are to be an extension of the work of the church that meets in a public building every Sunday. Again and again we read of people in the New Testament and 'the church that is in their house' (Rom. 16:5; Col. 4:15; Philem. 2). It is something that should be true of every Christian home.

1. Foster Christian fellowship

In these days of rapid urbanization, it is important to use our homes to foster Christian fellowship. Soon ninety per cent of the world's population will be living in huge cities and only ten per cent in rural areas. The frightening thing about this movement to the cities is that people do not get to know each other. They are lost among the vast masses, and they feel lonely and unwanted. This can happen in even the best of churches as well. People can come to a church for six months or a year and still remain unknown to the majority of the members. They may see each other but they never talk. They smile at each other but they never visit one another and get to know each other.

But do we not belong to one big family, the family of God? And are we not the children of God and brothers and sisters in Christ? And is it not God's will that we should know each other and care about each other? Paul says in Romans 15:7, 'Therefore receive one another, just as Christ also received us, to the glory of God', and again, 'Greet one another with a holy kiss.' (Rom. 16:6). It is our business to get to know each other. And we should seek every Sunday to speak to at least one person at church that we have not spoken to before or not spoken to for some time.

But because time after the services is limited, the next step is to invite people over to your house for a more relaxed time of conversation. If I read the situation correctly, there is a desperate need for Christians to open their front doors to others. Even if each Christian family shared a meal once a month with another Christian family it would be a good start toward fostering Christian fellowship.

2. Encourage spiritual growth in other Christians
Our homes can be used to encourage spiritual growth in other Christians. Statistics show that of all the people

who come to faith in Christ, those most likely to grow spiritually are those who live in a Christian home or are befriended in a Christian home. Indeed, this was the reason why John Wesley's converts in the eighteenth century were better discipled and consolidated in the faith than George Whitefield's. Both men preached in the open air or in large buildings but Wesley was more methodical and had his followers meet in homes every week for further instruction and nurture at the hands of lay preachers. Wesley's converts came to be called Methodists because although they worshipped in Anglican church buildings on Sundays, they used this new method of weekly meetings in homes to methodically apply God's Word to their daily lives. Actually the term Methodist was first applied for the same reason to the members of John Wesley's 'Holy Club' at Oxford University some years before.

As the movement grew and they sought to build their own houses of worship, the fire of Methodism began to die down and now in the English-speaking world its churches are becoming more and more liberal. But thank God, near the end of the twentieth century, the Holy Spirit began to lead people in many different denominations to bring Christian ministry back into Christian homes. Thousands and thousands of small mid-week Bible study and prayer groups are meeting in homes all over the world today, and people are finding great blessing in doing so.

People who once said that they could never pray in a church building among a lot of people have found that they can pray in a smaller meeting in someone's living-room. People who would never have expressed an opinion in a large Bible study group have found that in a home fellowship group, sitting around a table with a few friends, they are able to ask questions and contribute to the discussion. It is one of the wonderful movements of the Spirit of God in a fast-growing urban society. The Lord would surely like every Christian home to be open for times of prayer, Bible study and discussion. But there is something more.

3. Promote community evangelism

Our homes can be a blessing to the unconverted as they are used to promote community evangelism. Hospitality has converting power. A person is more likely to come to church and accept the gospel if they have first been in our home and met Christians there. There is nothing like meeting with Christians in their home to convince unbelievers that there is something real in Christianity. I truly believe that as a general rule, non-Christians should first be introduced to our homes before being introduced to our church. You will only get people to take you seriously if you befriend them in your home and if they know that you are not just being nice to them because you want to increase the numbers attending your church.

Is this not how many people come to faith? More often than not it is through a Christian truly befriending them. Sometime later when you have an opportunity to share the gospel with them, because they know you well and have come to trust in your desire for their welfare, they will take what you say seriously. That is the way to gain their respect and confidence and get a proper hearing for the gospel.

4. Accommodate God's servants

Our homes can also be used to accommodate God's servants. The early church was much more dependent on travelling preachers and teachers than we are. So the apostles made it very plain to the early Christians that it was their duty to accommodate these workers and send them on the next leg of their journey (Titus 3:13). The whole of the third epistle of John was written to this end. John writes:

> Beloved, you do faithfully whatever you do for the brethren and for strangers, who have borne witness of your love before the church. If you send them forward on their journey in a manner worthy of God, you will do well, because they went forth for his name's sake, taking nothing from the Gentiles. We therefore ought to receive such, that we may become fellow workers for the truth (3 John 5–8).

John is clear that Christians need to open their homes to visiting preachers or missionaries

EXPLANATION

who come to minister to their church. In doing so we are working with them for the proclamation of the truth in Jesus.

There is, however, one prohibition of hospitality in the New Testament. It is found in the second epistle of John. It is this: never give hospitality to a preacher of heresy. He is the only person you are not to accommodate in your home. For if he has twisted the Scriptures and is no longer preaching the gospel accurately, you will only help to spread his wicked ideas by accommodating him. John writes: 'If anyone comes to you and does not bring this doctrine, do not receive him into your house nor greet him; for he who greets him shares in his evil deeds' (2 John 10–11). But with that exception we are to welcome into our homes any true servant of God who needs accommodation and food. Every Christian home should be available for this. We live in an age when many people do not want others to get too close to them and then see their imperfections. The result is that in America it is now more common to accommodate visiting preachers or missionaries in motels than in people's homes. Let us break the cycle and start using our homes for the work of Jesus Christ.

THINK ABOUT IT

Holy families must be the chief preservers of the interest of religion in the world.
— Richard Baxter

THINK ABOUT IT

The family circle is the supreme conductor of Christianity.
— Henry Drummond

If Christ is in your house, your neighbours will soon know it.
— D. L. Moody

If family religion were duly attended to and properly discharged, I think the preaching of the Word would not be the common instrument of conversion.
— Richard Baxter

EXPLANATION

The manner of Christian hospitality

Let us now turn our attention to the manner in which Christian hospitality is to be given. There are three main considerations to be noted.

1. We are to offer hospitality without grumbling
1 Peter 4:9 says, 'Be hospitable to one another without grumbling.' In other words, we are to be hospitable without complaining about its cost to us in terms of finance, time, effort or lack of privacy. People quickly sense when we are more concerned about the amount of food they eat or the amount of time they are consuming than we are about them. Hospitality, after all, is concerned with people. People matter more than things. It

is the warmth of our love and the joy of sharing that makes hospitality such a blessing to others.

2. We are to offer hospitality without thought of reward
Hospitality is not to be confined to friends for whom we have a special affection. Neither are we to seek out only those of our own age group or social standing. Although it is good to give hospitality to our friends or peers, it can often be merely out of selfishness on our part and the personal enjoyment we get out of their company. Hospitality must also be extended to strangers, the Scriptures say (1 Tim. 5:10; Heb. 13:2).

In addition we must not only ask those who can ask us back again. True hospitality is never a business arrangement (if I invite you I hope you will invite me to your home). In fact our Lord told us to specialize in entertaining people who cannot repay us in kind. Jesus said,

> When you give a dinner or a supper, do not ask your friends, your brothers, your relatives, nor your rich neighbours, lest they also invite you back, and you be repaid. But when you give a feast, invite the poor, the maimed, the lame, the blind. And you will be blessed, because they cannot repay you; for you shall be repaid at the resurrection of the just (Luke 14:12–14).

It is the old story that if we pursue our reward from men and women here we will get it, but we must not look for a reward from God in the hereafter. Rather we are to open our homes without any expectation of the kindness being returned. We are to show hospitality for no other reason than to show God's kindness to others.

3. We are to offer hospitality that is worthy of God
As we offer hospitality we are to follow the encouragement of 3 John 6 that 'if you send them forward on their journey in a manner worthy of God, you will do well.' John assumes that Gaius will entertain the preachers who are coming to his church as he has done before. When their mission is over, John writes, speed them on their way to the next church with every comfort you can and provide for them 'in a manner worthy of God'. Therefore, we are to take care of every guest as if he were none other than God himself. We are to treat them with the best of our time, our thought and our means.

Please note that it is our best we must give not someone else's. It happens all too often that we hold back from hospitality because we feel that we cannot offer what others are able to offer. Our emphasis in hospitality is far more on the standard of our food and furniture than on the quality of our Christian love and fellowship, and so we withhold it. But would we shut Christ out, on the grounds that our home is too plain and humble for him? He came not to a king's palace but to a carpenter's cottage. The absence of money and splendour cannot bar us from entertaining Jesus Christ, the Lord of glory.

EXPLANATION

Well, then, if our home is not too humble for the King of kings, no lesser person should reject it because of its simplicity. On the contrary, the chief beauty of Christian hospitality is its simplicity. The simpler it is, the better. So if our hospitality is worthy of God we have no need to fear. What is good enough for him ought to be more than good enough for his people.

The reward of Christian hospitality

Hospitality was often rewarding to the hosts in the Old Testament. Abraham's guests brought him the wonderful news that at last he and Sarah were going to have a little boy of their own (Gen. 18:1–10). Elijah brought his hostess in Zarephath the present of a cruse of oil and a barrel of meal that never ran out through many months of famine. He also raised her son from the dead (1 Kings 17:8–24). The woman who added a room to her house for the prophet Elisha was handsomely rewarded when her son died and the preacher came and raised the boy back to life again (2 Kings 4:8–37).

Hospitality is rewarding. And I am not just thinking of a box of chocolates or an ornament or some other gift that we may thoughtfully give to our host. Our host is far better rewarded if, when we depart, our conversation and presence leaves behind something of the fragrance of our Lord Jesus Christ (2 Cor. 2:14–16; 3:5–6). Have we ever given that any thought? We give thought to our clothing when we go for a meal at a friend's home. But it is far more important that, as guests, we should prepare our hearts. It is much more important to make sure that our conversation and the whole demeanour of our personality are a joy to those who are kind enough to welcome us into their homes.

What a pity that we sometimes presume on other people's hospitality and leave nothing behind us but frivolity or negative criticism. We must be Christian guests as well as hosts. For God rewards Christian hospitality especially through our guests. Thus the Bible says, 'Do not forget to entertain strangers, for by so doing some have unwittingly entertained angels' (Heb. 13:2). Would it not be a shock if we got to heaven and an angel met us and said, 'You know, I came to your house one day.' We should not be so incredulous. It happened to Abraham. It also happened to Lot and to Gideon. Be hospitable to strangers 'for by doing so some have unwittingly entertained angels'.

But even if we do not entertain an actual angel, we never know what great blessing a Christian stranger's visit may bring to our home. One often reads of a child or a spouse being converted by the presence and testimony of a visiting missionary or preacher in their home. My wife and I have had our knowledge of biblical theology greatly enriched by having able expositors in our home while doing a Bible conference in the church where I was pastoring. In one-to-one discussions they cleared up difficulties in our understanding of the Bible that neither seminary nor books were able to do.

In our first pastorate we were called to plant a church just west of Johannesburg in an area where missionaries from three different overseas societies resided. Having them in our home kindled a passion to support and promote worldwide evangelism that I did not have before. Moreover, through the ministry of Christian hospitality, these missionaries were largely responsible for encouraging four of our young people to train for the mission field where they are still serving. God does reward us for using our homes for Christ.

Christian reader, are you 'given to hospitality' as the New Testament exhorts you to be? Are you a good steward of the home God has given to you? Is it a place where brothers and sisters in Christ can meet? Christian hospitality is one of the most precious things to be found in this world, and therefore it is one of the most valuable things a Christian is able to offer.

KEY THOUGHTS

Christian hospitality is a God-given gift that is too often undervalued and unemployed. We often pray for opportunities to witness to our friends and neighbours and yet overlook one of the best ways to do so: our home, however humble it may be. People, whether Christians or non-Christians are not as starved for food as they are for true friendship. They want someone to show genuine concern for them as a whole person and spend time and thought in reaching out to them. Our cities and towns are full of lonely people and a friendly, caring Christian home can be a

wonderful place to encourage them to open their
hearts to the Friend of sinners.

QUESTIONS FOR DISCUSSION

1. *Define Christian hospitality. Refer to Romans 12:13 and Hebrews 13:2.*

2. *What should a Christian's attitude be when entertaining other people? Read 1 Peter 4:9 and 3 John 6.*

3. *In what ways can God use a Christian's home to bring glory and honour to his name? See Luke 5:27–32; Acts 2:46–47; Romans 15:7 and 3 John 5–8.*

4. *Did Jesus promise a reward for being hospitable? What does Luke 14:12–14 say?*

5. *Have you been practising Christian hospitality on a regular basis? If not, consider ways in which you can begin such a ministry.*

SUGGESTIONS FOR PRAYER

1. *Thank Jesus Christ for his willingness to suffer and die on Calvary's cross to open his home in heaven for you.*

2. *Ask him to forgive you if you have not been using*

DISCUSS IT

PRAYER

your home as a place to befriend and help others for his sake.

3. *Pray for grace to begin practising hospitality, not grudgingly, without any thought of return from the recipients and in a manner worthy of God.*

A charge to keep I have,
    A God to glorify,
A never-dying soul to save,
    And fit it for the sky:

To serve the present age,
    My calling to fulfil,—
O may it all my powers engage
    To do my Master's will!

Arm me with jealous care,
    As in Thy sight to live;
And O, Thy servant, Lord, prepare
    A strict account to give.

Help me to watch and pray,
    And on Thyself rely,
And let me ne'er my trust betray,
    But press to realms on high.

— *Charles Wesley (1707–1788)*

CHAPTER TEN

THE ACCOUNTABILITY OF A STEWARD OF GOD

BIBLE REFERENCE

Work out your own salvation
with fear and trembling; for it is God
who works in you both to will and to do
for his good pleasure
(Phil. 2:12–13).

The subject of our divine stewardship is considered unpalatable precisely because none of us likes to know where we are falling short in our duty to God. The famous American statesman, Daniel Webster, was once asked what was the most important subject that had ever occupied his attention. His reply was, 'My personal responsibility.' No one should feel that more keenly than the Christian because he is a steward of the greatest of all masters, almighty God, his Creator and Redeemer. It does not matter whether the goods he has entrusted to us are great or small, our responsibility to God is our highest responsibility. Moreover, whether we like it or not that responsibility involves accountability. Our loving and generous Maker has endowed us all with physical life, time, talents and possessions and we cannot avoid being accountable to him for them.

So Paul reminds the Corinthians:

For we must all appear before the judgement
seat of Christ, that each one may receive the

things done in the body, according to what he has done, whether good or bad. Knowing, therefore, the terror of the Lord, we persuade men... We implore you on Christ's behalf, be reconciled to God (2 Cor. 5:10–11,20).

We have all failed God miserably. We have served our interests instead of his, which is the essence of sin. We need to be made right with God through Christ 'who knew no sin', but was 'made... sin for us, that we might become the righteousness of God in him' (2 Cor. 5:21). This reconciliation of sinners to God was effected when Jesus took our sins on himself and on the cross paid the penalty of death, which we deserved. He died there, says Paul, 'that those who live should live no longer for themselves, but for him who died for them and rose again' (2 Cor. 5:15). Paul repeats this warning in Romans 14:10,12: 'For we shall all stand before the judgement seat of Christ... then each of us shall give account of himself to God.'

Some of us, however, are very adept at shifting responsibility for our actions to someone else, like Adam who put the blame for his sin on Eve. It reminds me of the old man in the hospital who had been married for forty-five years. His wife was at his bedside when he turned to her and said, 'You know Martha, I've been thinking. Do you remember the first year we were married? We had a bad crop and lost half the farm, and there you were right by my side.' 'Yes', she replied. 'The next year', he went on, 'we had another bad crop and lost the other half of the farm, and there you were right by my

EXPLANATION

side.' 'Yes', she affirmed. 'And then we had ten kids', he said, 'and all of them wanted to go to college, but not one of them could get a scholarship. And there you were, right by my side.' 'Yes, dear', she smiled. 'Now I am dying here in the hospital', he whispered. 'The doctors don't expect me to walk out of here alive. Yet here you are right by my side. You know Martha, I believe you're bad luck!'

In Luke 16 our Lord told a parable to his disciples that began like this:

> There was a certain rich man who had a steward, and an accusation was brought to him that this man was wasting his goods. So he called him and said to him, 'What is this I hear about you? Give an account of your stewardship, for you can no longer be steward' (Luke 16:1–2).

Our Lord saw the future as a day of accounting — as a day of judgement — and every wise person will do the same. Samuel Johnson once remarked, 'I remember that my Maker has said that he will place the sheep on his right hand and the goats on his left. That is a solemn truth which this frivolous age needs to hear.' The frivolous age he was talking about was the eighteenth century, but there is still plenty of frivolity around.

Let us heed the warning of this parable of the unjust steward: 'What is this I hear about you?

Give an account of your stewardship.' The story itself is quite simple, but its message is a little puzzling. The rich man in verse 1 is an absentee landlord who had to employ a steward to take control of all his possessions. Unfortunately the steward used his position of trust to misappropriate his master's goods for his own benefit. In time, reports to that effect reached his master's hearing and he immediately called the steward to account and then told him to pack his bags and get off the estate as soon as possible.

As you can well imagine, this was a grave situation for the dishonest steward. His career was ruined. No one else would employ a man who was known to have stolen from his master. Starvation was staring him in the face. The steward, therefore, set out to prepare for the future as best he could. This is what he did. He alone knew who owed his master money or goods and how much. So the steward called all his master's debtors before him and made them debtors to himself by debiting them with far less than they owed. In other words, he changed the invoices. To the man who owed his master a hundred measures of oil (about 800 gallons or 3,000 litres) he said, 'Take your bill, and sit down quickly and write fifty.'

This the steward did with every one of his master's debtors. He put them in his debt so that he would have somewhere to live and someone from whom he could seek compensation. And it is here that our Lord brings his story to an unusual ending. He tells us that when the master was informed of the plot, he 'commended the unjust steward because he had dealt shrewdly'

(Luke 16:8). 'I may have a dishonest steward', says the master, 'but he is very shrewd. What a pity he has used his ingenuity in such a wicked way to get himself out of a terrible fix.' The master could not, obviously, approve of his steward's dishonesty, but he does recognize that the man is extremely clever when it comes to his own future welfare.

Jesus ends the parable by saying, 'For the sons of this world are more shrewd in their generation [literally, in dealing with their own kind] than the sons of light' (Luke 16:8). In other words the wicked are more clever at making a better life for themselves in this world than the righteous are at making a better future for themselves in the next world. Both the steward and his master's debtors were willing to be dishonest and to alter the bills for their mutual benefit. They were all in the evil scheme together. But 'the sons of light', says Jesus, do not show the same eagerness and ingenuity to use God's goods to help their fellow believers and thereby develop close bonds of love with them — bonds that will last through eternity. Let us now look at some of the lessons our Lord wants us to draw from the parable.

All we are and have is a trust from God

The truth that all we are and have is a trust from God is repeated throughout Scripture because it is one that we need to be constantly reminded of. We are stewards of God. Our abilities and possessions belong to him and are to be used for the benefit of his kingdom (to bring people into his kingdom and to enjoy all its marvellous blessings). It is sinful, therefore, when we say, 'This is mine I earned it', or, 'I am going to do what I want with my life.' It is sinful to talk like that because all the money that you have in your bank account, all your gifts and talents and all the material possessions that you control do not really belong to you. They belong to your almighty Creator. You are only a steward of them and you will have to give an account to God for the way that you have managed the property he has put in your care.

There is no ambiguity as to who the true owner of the world is. God declares in Psalm 50: 'For every beast of the forest is mine and the cattle on a thousand hills... For the world is mine, and all its fulness' (Ps. 50:10,12). The world is God's estate. Everything in it belongs to him and on the day of judgement we will be answerable to him if we have simply feathered our own nest instead of furthering his ends. We do have a benevolent Master 'who gives us richly all things to enjoy' (1 Tim. 6:17). But supremely, the wealth of his estate is to be used to advance his cause not ours.

Jesus says in Luke 16:12, 'And if you have not been faithful in what is another man's, who will give you what is your own?' It is another picture of the day of judgement. If, when God examines the books, it is found that we have been untrustworthy with his property in this life, he will not reward us with true riches of our own in heaven. That is our Lord's first application of this parable. Every earthly benefit that we have has been entrusted to us by our heavenly Master who desires that we should use them for his glory. But, make no mistake, one day we will have to give an account to him of how we have used his property.

Earthly assets are the least of all treasures because they will not last

In Luke 16, Jesus makes reference to unrighteous mammon. The word mammon is a transliteration of the Aramaic word for wealth or earthly assets in any shape or form. Our Lord calls it *unrighteous* mammon because it is the chief delight and desire of a selfish and unrighteous world. People live for earthly prizes instead of living for God. Our Lord is warning us to be wary of money, just as Paul does in 1 Timothy 6:10 when he says that 'the love of money is a root of all kinds of evil'. Money itself is not evil, but it is highly addictive — the more you have, the more you want. And like a drug, the craving is so powerful, you will soon do anything for it. Someone has called money the scariest drug on the market today.

Jesus, therefore, calls worldly wealth of any kind 'the mammon of unrighteousness' (as the

Greek literally reads) because it draws the worst out of men and leads to all kinds of selfish and evil behaviour. Jesus goes on to say, 'No servant can serve two masters; for either he will hate the one and love the other, or else he will be loyal to the one and despise the other. You cannot serve God and mammon' (Luke 16:13). When men covet an earthly prize it becomes an idol that they worship and serve. Mammon calls the tune and dictates the policy because it is the key to worldly success and pleasure. That is why the Bible condemns covetousness as idolatry. It is worshipping something other than God. That is why you cannot serve both God and mammon.

'Now', says Luke, 'the Pharisees who were lovers of money, also heard all these things, and they derided him' (Luke 16:14). The Pharisees considered themselves to be the true servants of God. But our Lord quickly informed them: 'God knows your hearts. For what is highly esteemed among men is an abomination in the sight of God' (Luke 16:15). People think worldly treasures are everything but God says that they are nothing unless they are used for his glory. One day God will destroy mammon along with all the evil it has produced. Of all the important things that a man or woman has to deal with in this life, money and temporal assets are the least important in the eyes of God. They are not to be ends in themselves but simply the means to the greatest end, namely the glory of God and the eternal good of our fellow human beings. Thus our Lord says, 'He who is faithful in what is least is faithful also in much; and he who is unjust in what is least, is unjust also in much' (Luke 16:10). Serving God by being Christlike and helping others is more important than becoming rich and famous and powerful at the expense of God.

Again, in verse 11 Jesus says, 'Therefore if you have not been faithful [to God] in the [use of] unrighteous mammon, who will commit to your trust the true riches?' Worldly assets are not true riches. They are only a stepping stone to true riches. Money is only a means to assist the needy and to rescue the lost for God. Mammon must never be the end. It is the least important thing in life. If God cannot even trust us with that which is least, how can he trust us with what he calls the 'true riches' (like the truth of the gospel, the gifts of the Spirit, prayer and service in and through his church)?

Now with this downplay of the importance of worldly assets you might be tempted to think that we should not care about them at all but rather give our attention completely to spiritual and heavenly things like prayer, meditation, worship and witness. But not so. For what Jesus is actually saying in verses 9 to 12 is that the way we manage the earthly riches God entrusts to us now will determine our true riches hereafter. Money may be a very little thing but it reveals, as nothing else can, our true spiritual condition. That is the point our Lord is making. He is saying that upon earth you are in charge of things that are not really yours. You cannot take them with you when you die. You are only a steward over them. They are little because you only have them for a little while. In heaven, however, you will get riches that are essentially and eternally yours. But what you will be given in heaven depends on how you used the lesser things that God put in your care on earth.

Now I must sound a note of caution here. Our Lord is not teaching that we can buy our way into heaven by trying to do a lot of good with money or by helping people in other ways. Salvation cannot be bought or earned. Indeed, Jesus says in Matthew 16:26 that there is nothing that a man can give in exchange for his own soul (to redeem or buy back his own lost soul). You can gain all the gold and silver in the world and all the other assets that people prize, and you still would not have enough to purchase one precious drop of Christ's blood without which, the Bible says, there can be no remission of sin (Heb. 9:22). Likewise, Peter says, 'You were not redeemed with corruptible things, like silver or gold... but with the precious blood of Christ' (1 Peter 1:18–19).

So Jesus is not saying that temporal riches can help you get into heaven. Rather, he is explaining that the human heart cannot use mammon in a God-glorifying way without being changed by the Holy Spirit. True, he does not say that explicitly here but this truth is stated elsewhere in the Word and is very clearly implied in this parable. Only the gift of the Holy Spirit at conversion can change our attitude to earthly treasures. When you see that changed attitude, when you observe how faithfully a man or woman uses the riches of this world to glorify God, then you know that the grace of God is at work in their life. That is the second lesson to be learnt from this parable: earthly assets are the least of all treasures because they will not last. They will pass away with the world. But God is interested in what we do with our assets here because they reveal our true spiritual condition and our trustworthiness or untrustworthiness in using the things that belong to him and are only entrusted to us for his glory (Rom. 11:36).

We should be preparing for the time when our earthly assets fail

Now we come to the heart of the parable. Our Lord does not admire the steward's dishonesty, which is what we tend to think at first glance. Rather, he calls him the *unjust* steward. Luke 16 verse 8 plainly says that 'the master commended the unjust steward because he had dealt shrewdly' (because he saw that he was going to be without a job and he prepared for the inevitable). He was forward looking and in a very ingenious but dishonest way he used his present opportunities for future gain. That is what we are to emulate about him: his diligence to prepare for the future, not his dishonesty.

The one absolute certainty in life is death. It is not a fact that will affect only a few of us or even most of us — *everyone* will face death. The Bible says, 'It is appointed for men to die once, but after this the judgement' (Heb. 9:27). 'Therefore', says Paul, 'we make it our aim... to be well-pleasing to him [the Lord]. For we must all appear before the judgement seat of Christ, that each one may receive the things done in the body... whether good or bad' (2 Cor. 5:9–10). Likewise our Lord, in the parable in Luke, condemns the sons of light because they know that they will have to die one day and leave all the prizes of this world behind, and yet unlike the unjust steward, they are not preparing for it. They have no plan as to how to use their present earthly assets for future heavenly gain.

The lesson is all too plain. If Christians would only put as much ingenuity into serving God's ends as worldly people put into serving their own ends, they would have a brighter future. Luke 16 verse 9 says, 'And I say to you, make friends for yourselves by unrighteous mammon, that when you fail [literally, when it fails], they may receive you into an everlasting home.' In other words, use all the goods of this world that God gives you (your money, your energy, your time, your abilities) to build the kingdom of God, and you will establish friendships that will survive death. You and those whom you influence for God will become members of an everlasting home.

Paul says much the same thing to Timothy:

Command those who are rich in this present age not to be haughty, nor to trust in uncertain riches but in the living God, who gives us richly all things to enjoy. Let them do good, that they be rich in good works, ready to give, willing to share, storing up for themselves a good foundation for the time to come, that they may lay hold on eternal life (1 Tim. 6:17–19).

Paul is affirming the same teaching as our Lord Jesus. The rich are to lay up treasures in heaven, not treasures on earth, by using all that God has entrusted to them to help others to enter his kingdom and be saved for all eternity.

THINK ABOUT IT

THINK ABOUT IT

O God, stamp eternity on my eyeballs!
— *Jonathan Edwards*

The real value of a thing is the price it will bring in eternity.
— *John Wesley*

There is a difference between being willing to go to heaven and wanting to stay on earth — and wanting to go to heaven while being willing to stay on earth.
— *David Pawson*

The gospel teaches us that while believers are not rewarded on account of their works, they are rewarded according to their works.
— *R. L. Dabney*

It is very important that the teaching of Jesus in this parable grips our souls. We desperately need to learn how to use money faithfully and ingeniously for the glory of God. That goes equally for any other assets God gives us in this life. If this unjust man was so shrewd and so zealous in securing a worldly future for himself, how much more should we be imaginative and enthusiastic in using our resources in a God-glorifying way that will secure our eternal future? For our Christian interests are far more important than the steward's worldly interests, our work for God is far more honourable than his work, our ultimate success is much more certain than his and our heavenly reward is much more glorious and enduring than his could ever be.

Do we understand that? Do we believe that winning others to Christ by our words and deeds is the main reason why God has given us all of our worldly goods? Of course, hard choices will have to be made every day. When there is a conflict between the claims of God and the claims of getting rich or famous, it will soon be evident whether God is Lord or mammon is lord. That is what Jesus boils it all down to in Luke 16:13. We all have limited resources. We cannot do everything, and because we cannot do everything, we have to make choices. In making a choice, we have to say no to one thing and yes to another. When God has a claim and getting on in the world has a claim, which claim is going to win? Who is important? Which one is Lord? That is what Jesus is asking, and it is a very serious matter.

For example, raising a family in a Christian way is costly. To go as a family to a church where the Word of

God is taught may entail more travel than we wish. Again, it may require home-schooling our children or paying more to send them to a good Christian school where they will be helped and not hindered in their spiritual development. And yet again, some sacrifices will have to be made if our neighbours and the world are going to be evangelized. These are decisions that have financial implications not only for this life but for the life to come. Will mother stay at home with the children or do we want more earthly comforts? Will we plunge into buying a vacation home, a jet ski or some other luxury or will we forego them sacrificially so that others may be won for Christ?

These are not easy choices to make, but our spiritual responsibilities and our use of money and energy are tied together — whether we realize it or not. Nor does it end when we reach the stage where we feel we can retire. For as long as we are endowed with earthly riches, God has not retired us from stewardship. It is no time to say, 'I have worked hard all my life, and now I am going to spend my days travelling and enjoying my hobbies.' No, there is still much to be done in the kingdom of God. There are full-time missionaries to be sent to the field and students at home and overseas who need to be put through seminary. There are poor people in our church and in our community who need assistance. There are Christian books and tracts and tapes to give to those who could be saved or edified by them. The ways in which we can personally advance God's kingdom are legion, if only we had the concern and ingenuity to think of them.

After Jesus had told this parable and explained it, Luke says, 'The Pharisees who were lovers of money, also heard all these things, and they derided him' (Luke 16:14). They prided themselves on being pragmatic and successful. And the world still admires those who have become rich and powerful and famous. But 'what is highly esteemed among men', says Jesus, 'is an abomination [is detestable] in the sight of God' (Luke 16:15). The final audit still awaits us. What are we going to say to our heavenly Master when he opens the books to show us what we have done with the goods that are his?

◖KEY▐THOUGHTS◗

It is impossible to believe that we can be given so much by God our Creator and Redeemer and not be held account-able on the day of judgement for what we have done with it. In seven out of thirty-nine of his parables our Lord focuses solely on our accountability at the end of this life. It is foolish to ignore these solemn warnings and live as if a happy and prosperous life on earth is all that matters at this moment.

―――

Belief in the immortality of the soul and belief in the account-ability of the soul are fundamental beliefs in all religion.
— *J. Oswald Sanders*

DISCUSS IT

QUESTIONS FOR DISCUSSION

1. Read Luke 16:1–13 and answer the following questions:
   a. Why is the unjust steward commended?
   b. What is mammon and why is it called unrighteous?
   c. What are the true riches Jesus speaks of?
   d. Why can we not serve God and mammon?

2. Examine your life in the light of Luke 16:9,19–30. Can you think of anyone who will be glad to see you in heaven because of your faithful stewardship?

3. Use Matthew 25:14–46, 1 Corinthians 3:9–15 and 1 Timothy 6:17–19 to help you draw up a list of some of the things that you are doing to serve Christ and his people.

4. Will good intentions count when we are judged on the last day? See 2 Corinthians 5:10 and James 2:14–26.

PRAYER

SUGGESTIONS FOR PRAYER

1. Praise God for his justice and thank him that his judgement on the last day will be fair and based on all the facts.

2. *Confess with shame the number of times you have been unjust in your stewardship and used your Master's goods mainly for your own temporal benefit.*

3. *Pray for the strength and wisdom of the Holy Spirit to use your God-given resources in the best possible way for his greater glory.*

When Jesus comes to reward His servants,
    Whether it be noon or night,
Faithful to Him will He find us watching,
    With our lamps all trimmed and bright?

If, at the dawn of the early morning,
    He shall call us one by one,
When to the Lord we restore our talents,
    Will He answer us, 'Well done'?

Have we been true to the trust He left us?
    Do we seek to do our best?
If in our hearts there is naught condemns us,
    We shall have a glorious rest.

Blessed are those whom the Lord finds watching,
    In His glory they shall share;
If He shall come at the dawn or midnight,
    Will He find us watching there?

Oh, can we say we are ready, brother,
Ready for the soul's bright home?
Say, will He find you and me still watching,
Waiting, watching when the Lord shall come?

— *Fanny J. Crosby (1820–1915)*

THE GUIDE

CHAPTER ELEVEN

THE
WATCHFULNESS
OF A STEWARD
OF GOD

BIBLE REFERENCE

And the Lord said, 'Who then is that faithful and wise steward, whom his master will make ruler over his household, to give them their portion of food in due season? Blessed is that servant whom his master will find so doing when he comes. Truly, I say to you that he will make him ruler over all that he has' (Luke 12:42–44).

R. A. Torrey, the great American evangelist and Bible scholar of the early twentieth century, says in his book *What the Bible Teaches*, 'The imminent return of our Lord is the great Bible argument for a pure, unselfish, devoted, unworldly active life of service.' That sums up perfectly the lesson Jesus conveys in his parable of the watchful servants in Luke 12:35–48. The whole chapter is about covetousness and our idolatrous preoccupation with preserving our physical life and all the material comforts that enhance it.

Our Lord is careful to acknowledge to his disciples that food and clothing are a necessary part of human life in this world. He says, 'Your Father knows that you need these things' (Luke 12:30). Our main concern, however, should not be to lay up treasure on earth. That was the mistake of the farmer in the parable of the rich fool earlier in Luke 12. He had provided for the future as far as this life was concerned, but he had not taken

into account the life to come where his earthly possessions would be of no use to him at all. Our goal, rather,
should be to serve God's interests and thereby lay up
for ourselves 'treasure in the heavens that does not fail,
where no thief approaches nor moth destroys' (Luke
12:33). That is what Christ means in verse 21 when he
speaks about being 'rich toward God', and it should
always be the great concern of those who are his disciples. They are to live primarily for God.

C. S. Lewis wisely noted: 'If you read history you will
find that the Christians who did most for the present
world were precisely those who thought most of the next.'
Prime examples of this in the last two centuries are
Lord Shaftesbury, who revolutionized Britain's approach
to the mentally ill, the homeless, women and children
working in coal mines and children working in facto-
ries; Thomas Barnardo who set up a wonderful network
of orphanages; Elizabeth Fry who triggered widespread
prison reforms; William Wilberforce who brought about
the abolition of the slave trade in Britain and Jean Henri
Dunant who wrote a book that led to the founding of
the International Red Cross. These great figures of recent
history were all Christians who spent their lives serving
God according to his Word and their conscience. They
brought great blessing to this present world precisely
by laying up great treasure for the next.

Our Lord's remarks, therefore, are directed specifically
to his disciples; to those who follow him and 'seek the
kingdom of God' (Luke 12:31). 'Do not fear, little flock',
he says to them in verse 32, 'for it is your Father's good
pleasure to give you the kingdom.' In the parable Jesus

tells us how to overcome covetousness in a materialistic world and become rich toward God (Luke 12:35–38). It all has to do with our attitude. How should we look at life?

We are to see ourselves as servants waiting for the return of Jesus

Jesus tells us in this parable that he is our Master, and that he has left his household on earth to go to a wedding (that is to say, to make wedding arrangements). This is a frequent theme in our Lord's parables and it is important to understand Eastern wedding customs to appreciate the scene being portrayed. Betrothal was the first social procedure leading to marriage in biblical times, and it was a much more serious step than our modern custom of engagement. The marriage was arranged by the parents, and after the terms of the relationship were agreed on before witnesses, the bride and groom were committed to each other by oath.

There was typically an interval between the betrothal and the actual wedding to give the groom time to pay a dowry to the father of the bride. Jacob was required to work for Laban for seven years to receive Rachel as his bride (Gen. 29:18). Only when the dowry was paid, could the wedding feast proceed and the bride be claimed. The groom and his companions would then

EXPLANATION

proceed to the bride's house and escort her back to his home for the wedding feast.

That is the background to this parable. Our Master has gone away to make arrangements with God the Father for the greatest wedding ever. Of course, no parable can present every aspect of salvation because its purpose is simply to convey one key point. So in this parable the Christians who are left in Christ's household on earth are not presented as his waiting bride but as his servants because our Lord is focusing not on the great joys that await us at the marriage feast in heaven but on the serious spiritual responsibilities that confront us here on earth. The one we love and serve has gone away on very important business and left us in charge of his household. More importantly, Jesus has left us to wait for his return and we do not know how long this urgent business will detain him.

The Romans divided the night into four three-hour watches for sentry duty. Jesus says that the master could return in the second or in the third watch (Luke 12:38) — in other words, in the early hours of the morning. Moreover at night the house was locked from the inside to keep out burglars, which would mean that no matter how unearthly the hour of his return, the master was dependent on his servants to let him in. To be caught asleep at such an hour would be a very serious matter. The master would be tired and hungry and in no mood to be kept waiting at the door.

Likewise it is the duty of every servant of God to be ready for Christ's return. Jesus says,

EXPLANATION

Let your waist be girded and your lamps burning; and you yourselves be like men who wait for their master, when he will return from the wedding, that when he comes and knocks they may open to him immediately. Blessed are those servants whom the master, when he comes, will find watching... And if he should come in the second watch, or come in the third watch, and find them so, blessed are those servants. But know this, that if the master of the house had known what hour the thief would come, he would have watched and not allowed his house to be broken into. Therefore you also be ready, for the Son of Man is coming at an hour you do not expect (Luke 12:35–40).

The Christian life is future oriented. Five times we are commanded by Jesus in this parable to be ready or watching for his return to earth. Our eyes are to scan the horizon for the first signs of his coming. We are not to be preoccupied with the things of time and sense as the world is. Our hope is to be fixed on the future. That has been true for all of God's people right from the time of Adam. For when Adam believed Satan's lie and fell into sin, God promised that through the woman he would provide men and women a deliverer who would crush the serpent's head (Gen. 3:15). So Adam was a believer who looked

forward to the coming of the Son of Man. His hopes
were centred on the promised Messiah.

Throughout the Old Testament we find God's people
waiting expectantly for the coming of Christ. It is the
story of Enoch and Abraham, Moses and David, Isaiah
and all the other prophets up to the birth of Jesus. Even
in Luke's day he tells us of Simeon who was 'waiting
for the Consolation of Israel' (Luke 2:25). God had
promised Simeon that he would see the Messiah before
he died and he had now grown old waiting. But when
Mary and Joseph brought the baby Jesus to the temple
Simeon recognized him and said, 'Lord, now you are
letting your servant depart in peace... For my eyes have
seen your salvation' (Luke 2:29–30). Again, when Anna
the prophetess saw Jesus in Mary's arms, 'she gave thanks
to the Lord, and spoke of him to all those who looked
for redemption in Jerusalem' (Luke 2:38).

This attitude of expectation continues throughout the
New Testament, for although Jesus Christ came 2,000
years ago, the people of God now 'eagerly wait for him [to]
appear a second time, apart from sin, for salvation' (Heb.
9:28). The New American Standard Bible reads that he
'will appear a second time for salvation without reference
to sin, to those who eagerly await him'. For our Lord's first
visit was just a brief thirty years or so in which he took
our humanity upon himself in order that he might take
our sin and bear in his own body on the cross God's just
condemnation of it. 'Christ died for our sins according to
the Scriptures', says Paul, 'and... he rose again the third
day according to the Scriptures' (1 Cor. 15:3–4). On the
fortieth day Jesus ascended into heaven where he is now

EXPLANATION

seated at the right hand of the Father from where he will come to claim his bride (Mark 16:19). That is to say, his return is to complete the salvation of his people. So on the eve on his death Jesus said to his disciples, 'Let not your heart be troubled; you believe in God, believe also in me... I go to prepare a place for you. And if I go and prepare a place for you, I will come again and receive you to myself; that where I am, there you may be also' (John 14:1–3). Moreover, when Jesus ascended into heaven, two angels said to his disciples, 'This same Jesus who was taken up from you into heaven, will so come in like manner as you saw him go into heaven' (Acts 1:11).

Christians, then, are those who are eagerly waiting for the second coming of Christ to complete their salvation. So if we are only living for the here and now we have reason to question our salvation. Paul says to the Thessalonians, 'You turned to God from idols to serve the living and true God, and to wait for his Son from heaven, ... even Jesus who delivers us from the wrath to come' (1 Thess. 1:9–10). Do you long for the return of Jesus? Can your life be described as one of anticipation for that event? Does his coming affect your behaviour and service? Are you obsessed about earthly things, about what you will eat or what clothes you will wear? Christians should not be preoccupied with these things. Our great, our supreme interest is to be ready for the return of our Master. And the best way to be ready for his return is to be busy in his service. 'When the cat's away, the mice will play' is worldly thinking not Christian thinking. Just as an employee does his best work when he expects his boss to arrive at any moment, so the more we live in expectation of Christ's sudden return, the more conscientious and industrious we will be.

A lady once asked John Wesley, 'Suppose you knew you were to die at 12 o'clock tomorrow night, how would you spend the intervening time?' 'Why, madam', he replied, 'just as I intend to spend it now. I should preach this night at Gloucester and again at 5 tomorrow morning. After that I should ride to Tewkesbury, preach in the afternoon, and meet the societies in the evening. I should then repair to friend Martin's house, who expects to entertain me, retire to my room at 10 o'clock, commend myself to my heavenly Father, lie down to rest, and wake up in glory.' That, too, is how best to await the return of our Lord Jesus Christ. As one hymnwriter put it:

O happy servant he,
    In such employment found!
He shall His Lord with rapture see
    And be with honour crowned.

We are to be ready for Christ to return at any moment

In verse 39 of the parable in Luke 12 our Lord says, 'But know this, that if the master of the house had known

EXPLANATION

what hour the thief would come, he would have watched and not allowed his house to be broken into.' It is a very simple analogy. If thieves were required to send us notice when they were coming to our house, we would be ready to guard our home at that hour. The fact is, however, that people are robbed at a time when they are not expecting it (when they are either not at home or sound asleep).

Jesus is comparing his return to the earth to a thief robbing a house. He is going to come at a time when nobody is expecting his arrival. The fact that no one knows the exact time when Jesus will return is repeated over and over again in the New Testament. In Mark 13 Jesus says that the Son of Man will come 'in the clouds with great power and glory... But of that day and hour', he goes on, 'no one knows, neither the angels in heaven, nor the Son, but only the Father. Take heed, watch and pray; for you do not know when the time is.' (Mark 13:26, 32–33). In 2 Peter 3:10 the apostle says, 'But the day of the Lord will come as a thief in the night.' In 1 Thessalonians 5:2 Paul says the same thing: 'For you yourselves know perfectly that the day of the Lord so comes as a thief in the night.' And then at the end of the New Testament Jesus says, 'Behold, I am coming as a thief. Blessed is he who watches and keeps his garments [or, who is dressed and ready to meet me]' (Rev. 16:15).

Now with such repeated warnings it is amazing that throughout the history of the church people have tried to predict when Christ would come. Even in the past 100 years Mormons, Jehovah's Witnesses, Seventh Day Adventists and even some evangelical Christian authors have made several unsuccessful predictions. Each time that Jesus did not come the same predictable answers were given. The so-called prophets claimed that either he came and nobody saw him, or they did not quite get the day right because some other factors elsewhere in the Bible were not taken into account.

Christians must not be deceived by these false prophets. No one knows the year or the month or the day or the hour of Christ's coming. And part of the reason why no one knows is that Jesus wants us to work conscientiously and industriously as those who believe his return could surprise us at any moment. He does not want us to be tempted into loafing for it is the labourer, not the loafer, who is worthy of his hire. Anna and Simeon were ready for Christ's first coming because they were faithfully doing the tasks assigned for them in the temple. They were in the right place, doing the right thing as far as God was concerned. They did not take off work for extra sleep or to get drunk (Luke 12:45). When Jesus came to the temple, they were there doing the job the Lord asked them to do. Anna and Simeon were ready to welcome Jesus and joyfully receive him in their arms precisely because they were at their post of duty.

Now the same applies to us. Jesus says, 'Who then is that faithful and wise steward, whom his master will

EXPLANATION

make ruler over his household, to give them their portion of food in due season? Blessed is that servant whom his master will find so doing when he comes' (Luke 12:42–43). That is how to be ready for our Master's return. We are to be doing the job he has assigned us in his household. Verse 35 also makes this clear: 'Let your waist be girded.' Why? Because the long flowing robes of those days were not conducive to work. When a man prepared for work he would gather up his robe under his girdle so that he could move without encumbrance. Moreover, says Jesus, 'Let… your lamps be burning.' Why? Because when night falls you cannot work in the darkness. It is all about being busy and not loafing or sleeping. Watchfulness for our Lord's return is the best antidote to idleness or wickedness. For when Christ appears we want to face him with 'confidence and not be ashamed before him at his coming' (1 John 2:28). Jesus says, 'And you yourselves be like men who wait for their master, when he will return from the wedding, that when he comes and knocks they may open to him immediately' (Luke 12:36).

THINK ABOUT IT

That day lies hid that every day we be on the watch.
— *Augustine*

Christ hath told us he will come, but not when, that we might never put off our clothes, or put out the candle.
— *William Gurnall*

The fact that Jesus Christ is to come again is not a reason for star-gazing, but for working in the power of the Holy Ghost.
— *C. H. Spurgeon*

Christ's watchful servants will be rewarded

In Luke 12 verse 37 our Lord says, 'Blessed are those servants whom the master, when he comes, will find watching.' And at the end of verse 38 he says again, 'Blessed are those servants.' Here is another beatitude from the lips of Jesus. It is a blessing promised to those who patiently watch for his second coming. What is the blessing that is promised? Jesus declares, 'Assuredly, I say to you that he will gird himself and have them sit down to eat, and will come and serve them' (Luke 12:37). What amazing condescension! What unsurpassed love and kindness! No human master would be expected to do this for us, let alone our divine Master.

In the days of Jesus, when a master arrived home late at night after a long journey, he would give his donkey to one servant and say, 'Take him to the stable and give him some fodder.' Then he would turn to another servant and say, 'Prepare me some food and get my bed ready.' Even though they had been working right through the day and into the night the servants would be expected to wait on their master. But in this parable when the master arrives home tired and hungry in the early hours of the morning, what does he do? Jesus Christ, the Lord of glory, girds *himself* for work and tells his servants to sit down and enjoy some well-deserved rest while he prepares the food and serves *them*.

That is the kind of God and Master we serve and that is an aspect of the glory of heaven God's Word will not allow us to overlook. If the love of God sets us to work, the God of love will find us the wages. True, we are the servants of Jesus, and when we get to heaven we are going to serve him in a place where there is no night (Rev. 22:3,5). It is going to be non-stop worship (Rev. 7:15). We are going to cast our crowns before him and worship him with all our heart and strength. Whatever he bids we are going to do. But the other side of Christ's return and the glory of heaven is that he will wait on us. He will sit us down to eat at 'the marriage supper of the Lamb', which will last for all eternity. He will wipe away our tears and soothe our weary limbs. We will neither hunger anymore nor thirst anymore. From his right hand we will enjoy pleasures for evermore (Rev. 7:16–17; 21:4; Ps.16:11).

This is what Jesus is referring to in this parable. The word translated as serve is the verb form of the noun deacon. Jesus will act as a deacon for those servants of his who watch for his return and are busy doing what he has assigned them to do.

Jesus did this at his first coming when on the eve of his crucifixion he took a towel and girded himself and began to wash his disciples' tired and dirty feet. He became the Servant of his servants and even died on the cross for them, offering himself as a ransom for their sins. And Jesus says that he is going to do this again. When he returns, the Son of God himself is going to serve his servants and give them indescribable comforts and delights. 'It is not lost labour to serve God', said John Calvin, 'for he has promised us a plentiful reward, and we shall not be disappointed in our expectation.' Endorsing this, C. H. Spurgeon said, 'God is a sure paymaster, though he does not always pay at the end of every week.'

Are you a watchful servant of Jesus? Are you free of covetousness and worldliness? Is your life dominated by the kind of work Christ wants to find you doing when he returns? Do you want the blessing of this beatitude? Do you want to sit at the marriage supper of the Lamb and be the recipients of all the delights of heaven? The only ones who will sit at that banquet are those who 'serve the living and true God, and wait for his Son from heaven, whom he raised from the dead, even Jesus who delivers us from the wrath to come' (1 Thess. 1:9–10). In the parable of the ten virgins, the five foolish virgins who were not ready to welcome the bridegroom were excluded from the wedding feast. Let us not be so foolish. Festive occasions with those we dearly love are good times not to be missed. Let us be wise and found ready at our post of duty for the approaching 'marriage supper of the Lamb' (Rev. 19:9).

KEY THOUGHTS

KEY THOUGHTS

We live in an age when the personal, visible return of the Lord Jesus Christ in power and great glory to judge all men (the living and the dead) is either denied or omitted from the preaching in many pulpits. The result is that too many church members think that life is just about raising a family, enjoying yourself and then, to top it all, going to heaven. There is little thought of faithfully serving their heavenly Master on earth in the duties of his household so that they may be ready and unashamed at his second coming. Whether it be near or far, it is the servant who stays at his post of duty who will be ready for Christ's return.

———

When Jesus comes there will be instant job satisfaction for us.
—*David N. Jones*

DISCUSS IT

QUESTIONS FOR DISCUSSION

1. *Do you believe that Jesus Christ is going to personally and visibly return one day in power and great glory to the earth? Find at least three New Testament references to substantiate your answer.*

2. *What will Jesus Christ do when he comes to the earth for a second time? For your answers refer to*

Matthew 25:31–46; Luke 12:41–48; 2 Peter 3:10–14.

3. *If Christ was to return today or if you had to die today, could you identify with these words in 1 Thessalonians 2:19, 2 Timothy 4:6–8 and 1 John 2:18? If you have any uncertainty examine your heart before God and put it right.*

SUGGESTIONS FOR PRAYER

1. *Thank Jesus Christ that he is faithful and true to his promise; that he is going to return to earth to judge the wicked and reward the righteous.*

2. *Confess your failure to serve him faithfully and ask for his forgiveness for neglected duties and squandered resources.*

3. *Ask him for the help of the Holy Spirit to resist coveting worldly riches and pleasures and to be diligent in fulfilling the duties he has assigned to you.*

O for a heart to praise my God,
    A heart from sin set free;
A heart that's sprinkled with the blood
    So freely shed for me.

A heart resigned, submissive, meek;
    My great Redeemer's throne;
Where only Christ is heard to speak,
    Where Jesus reigns alone.

A humble, lowly, contrite heart,
    Believing, true and clean,
Which neither life nor death can part
    From Him that dwells within.

A heart in every thought renewed
    And full of love divine,
Perfect and right and pure and good;
    A copy, Lord, of Thine.

Thy nature, gracious Lord, impart;
    Come quickly from above;
Write Thy new name upon my heart,
    Thy new, best name of love.

— *Charles Wesley (1707–1788)*

CHAPTER TWELVE

THE HUMILITY
OF A STEWARD
OF GOD

LOOK IT UP

I say... to everyone who is among you, not to think of
himself more highly than he ought to think,
but to think soberly, as God has dealt to each one
a measure of faith (Rom. 12:3).

So you also, when you have done everything
you were told to do, should say, 'We are unworthy
servants; we have only done our duty'
(Luke 17:10, NIV).

INTRODUCTION

The greatest temptation facing a faithful steward
of God is pride concerning his or her devotion to
and accomplishments for the kingdom of God.
It is natural for us to think more highly of ourselves than we ought, and Paul warns us precisely
against this temptation in Romans 12:3 when he
calls us to give ourselves to God's service. The
seed of self-importance was first planted in the
human heart in the garden of Eden by Satan himself, the proudest of all God's former servants.
For as Augustine so clearly stated, 'It was pride
that changed angels into devils; it is humility
that makes men as angels.' Unfortunately Eve
ate the forbidden fruit because she really
believed the devil's lie that she could become as
wise and great as God by doing so. And ever since,
human beings have been filled with self-love
and self-esteem.

Indeed, self-admiration is so natural to our fallen condition that only God can cure it. I am happy to say that by the grace of Jesus Christ God's remedy for human pride begins to take effect the moment we are converted and become new creatures. But the deep root of the false and inflated view we have of ourselves will only be completely eradicated from our bodies when we are glorified at the resurrection. Until then, pride is something that we will have to fight every moment of our lives. That is the only way we are to think of ourselves, says Paul in Romans 12:3, 'I say... to everyone who is among you, not to think of himself more highly than he ought to think, but to think soberly, as God has dealt to each one a measure of faith.'

You cannot be excluded from this directive. Paul is addressing this command to every Christian, and 'the measure of faith' he is speaking about here, is God's measuring stick of faith by which everyone is to evaluate themselves. What is that measuring stick? It is the Christian faith or the gospel that measures all men and women — *the standard of Christ's life and service.* Against that standard we are rebellious and guilty sinners who can only be forgiven and reconciled to God by Christ bearing our condemnation for us. In other words, we can only think soberly when we see ourselves in the light of Calvary's cross as nothing but hell-deserving sinners. No wonder Spurgeon said, 'The higher a man is in grace, the lower he will be in his own estimation.'

But it is not only the apostle Paul who warns Christians against thinking more highly of themselves than they ought to think, our Lord did so also. In Luke

17:1–10 Jesus is speaking to his disciples (to all believers) about the duties of the Christian life. On the one hand they are not to lead others to do wrong. On the other hand if anyone wrongs them they are to rebuke them, and if they repent of their wrongdoing they are to forgive them. Jesus says, 'And if he [your brother] sins against you seven times in a day, and seven times in a day returns to you, saying, "I repent," you shall forgive him' (Luke 17:4).

This is a tough standard to live by, and the apostles immediately saw that they needed a lot more faith in God than they had to be able to forgive like that. So they said to the Lord, 'Increase our faith' (Luke 17:5). But Jesus assures them that the secret of true godliness lies not in the *measure* of a person's faith but in it's *genuineness*. If our trust truly rests in God, the power to do the will of God will follow. Because it is not so much *great* faith in God that is required as *real* faith in a great God. 'So the Lord said, "If you have faith as a mustard seed [the tiniest of seeds], you can say to this mulberry tree, 'Be pulled up by the roots and be planted in the sea,' and it would obey you"' (Luke 17:5). The rabbis regarded the mulberry tree as the most firmly-rooted tree in Palestine. To uproot it is extremely difficult. Our Lord, however, is clearly not suggesting that his followers occupy themselves with pointless, difficult things like transferring a mulberry tree into the sea. His concern is with having true faith to do the difficult things that God requires of us. Nothing is impossible with faith if it is exercised within God's will.

But this is where the problem arises, for when men have the faith to do great things for God, they may fall victim to spiritual pride. It is to counteract all thought of pride, which is an abomination to God (Prov. 6:16–17), that Jesus goes on to remind his disciples that they are but servants. He says,

> And which of you, having a servant plowing or tending sheep, will say to him when he has come in from the field, 'Come at once and sit down to eat'? But will he not rather say to him, 'Prepare something for my supper, and gird yourself and serve me till I have eaten and drunk, and afterward you will eat and drink'? Does he thank that servant because he did the things that were commanded him? I think not. So likewise you, when you have done all those things which you are commanded, say, 'We are unprofitable servants. We have done what was our duty to do' (Luke 17:7–10).

Let us now consider what Jesus was trying to teach his disciples through this example.

A warning against spiritual pride

Quite simply Jesus is warning us against spiritual pride. The worst form of pride is not that which feels

EXPLANATION

superior to another human being. The worst form of pride is that which exalts itself at the expense of God, and the way that we most commonly do this is to think that God owes us something. This is the deepest and most wicked form of pride: to believe that human beings have rights that God is bound to honour.

In the West we live in democracies where everyone has certain 'inalienable rights', and it is very difficult, if not impossible, for us to see that God has *absolute* rights over his creatures. It offends our sense of social justice to think that any one could have the right to demand from us whatever they please. But that is precisely the authority God has over us as our Creator. 'It is he who has made us, and not we ourselves', says the psalmist (Ps. 100:3). Every talent or ability that we have was designed by God to serve his purposes in this world. We have no right to use them purely for ourselves.

Not only that, it is God alone who daily sustains us. Our breath comes from God. Our energy comes from God. Whatever we are able to do, we do in the physical and spiritual strength that God supplies. To think that I have time or energy or skills or interests above my Master's is both arrogant and untrue. God has every right to demand of us whatever he wants at every moment in our lives. That is what it means to be a steward or servant of God, says Jesus. Indeed, Jesus says in Luke 17:9 that nothing would shock and surprise the servant more than to have his master say to him, 'Thank you. You have worked hard; let me now serve you!' It is the duty of the servant to serve his master from the moment he gets up in the morning to the moment he goes to bed at night.

God is not indebted to us in any way

But there is something else that our Lord is teaching us in this illustration or parable and it is this: we can do nothing to make God feel indebted to us. It is very interesting that in this story there is no hint at all of any flaw in this man's service to his master. Jesus is giving us a picture of someone who is absolutely faithful and diligent in his service. He goes out early in the morning, and he does exactly what his master asks of him. He works very hard ploughing a field or tending a flock of sheep. Then when he returns to the homestead at sunset, he gladly prepares a meal and serves it to his master. He has not failed to do anything that his master required of him. He has worked very hard and very efficiently all day long.

But in verse 9 Jesus says, 'Does he [the master] thank that servant because he did the things that were commanded him? I think not.' He is simply doing what is expected of him. The master has no sense of gratitude, no sense of being indebted to his servant. He has only done what he should have done. He has not gone beyond the call of duty. Now if this seems strange and harsh to us, it is only because in our fallen, sinful condition we

EXPLANATION

keep thinking of God as a man and our service to him as service to an equal. But that is never how the true servants of God think, whether in the Old Testament or the New.

In Job 22:2–3 Eliphaz says to Job who is protesting his innocence,

Can a man be profitable to God,
Though he who is wise may be profitable to himself?
Is it any pleasure to the Almighty that you are righteous?
Or is it gain to him that you make your ways blameless?

The answer, of course, is an emphatic 'No!' God cannot benefit in any way from us, not even if we lived a sinless life. We would simply be living as God created us to live. How could we ever imagine that God could be indebted to us for that? How could it ever enter our mind that we deserve some reward from God for doing what we ought to do?

Paul says the same thing in Romans 11:35 (quoting again from Job): "'Or who has first given to him [God] and it shall be repaid to him?' For of him and through him and to him are all things, to whom be glory forever. Amen.' No human being, not even Adam before he sinned, has ever lived in such a way as to put God in his debt. The Bible from beginning to end says that it is impossible. We are always in the position of trying to repay God for what he has done for us. We do not expect God to thank us for thanking him for ransoming us from the wretched slavery of sin and promoting us to his glorious service. Our service for God is at best unsatisfactory, and so we always feel that we cannot do enough to show God how much we appreciate serving him whose service is perfect freedom (James 1:25).

In Romans 4:2 Paul says, 'For if Abraham was justified by works [by living a sinless life], he has something of which to boast.' Boast about to whom? He would be boasting to you and to me because we have never lived a sinless and perfect life, and he would be one up on us. 'But not before God', says Paul. He would have no claim on God. God would owe him nothing. Paul continues: 'For what does the Scripture say? "Abraham believed God, and it was accounted to him for righteousness." Now to him who works, the wages are not counted as grace but as debt' (Rom. 4:3–4). Abraham was the recipient of grace. He had not put God in his debt but he was heavily indebted to God instead.

The same was true of the apostles whom Jesus was teaching. What great things the apostles did for Jesus Christ. They won great multitudes for him. They suffered persecution and hardships for the gospel, and eventually most, if not all, were martyred for Christ. But all alike recognized that their best service did not give them any claim on God. All their labours were only possible by the grace of God as Paul freely acknowledges in 1 Corinthians 15:9–10:

EXPLANATION

For I am the least of the apostles, who am not worthy to be called an apostle, because I persecuted the church of God. But by the grace of God I am what I am, and his grace toward me was not in vain; but I laboured more abundantly than they all, yet not I, but the grace of God which was with me.

This is how you and I must feel about all we do for God during our entire lifetime. It is by grace that we have been called to serve God and he enables us to do so. 'So likewise you', says Jesus (Luke 17:10), 'when you have done all those things which you are commanded, say, "We are unprofitable servants. We have done what was our duty to do."'

THINK ABOUT IT

The surest mark of true conversion is humility.
— *J. C. Ryle*

Humility is pure honesty.
— *Jack McAlister*

Humility is the grace which lies prostrate at God's footstool, self-abasing and self-disparaging, amazed at God's mercy and abhorring its own vileness.
— *James Hamilton*

Humility is not a Sunday frock, but a workaday smock.
— *J. Oswald Sanders*

How God views our service for him

Jesus is not saying that God is unmindful and unappreciative of our service for him. He is not portraying God as a master who is demanding and hard to get along with. A parable, of necessity, has to focus on the main lesson being taught. Very few illustrations can present both sides of a truth at the same time. So, for the other side of the picture, we must go back to the parable in Luke 12 that we looked at in the previous chapter. There our Lord says, 'Blessed are those servants whom the master, when he comes, will find watching. Assuredly, I say to you that he will gird himself and have them sit down to eat, and will come and serve them' (Luke 12:37).

There is no contradiction here. Luke 17 is Christ's picture of how we are always to look on ourselves as 'unprofitable servants' who, because of our sinful state, can do nothing to put God in our debt. Luke 12, on the other hand, is Christ's picture of how God looks on our service. He looks on us with grace and appreciates our faithful service even though we are only doing our duty.

This is also the teaching of the parable of the talents in Matthew 25 when on the day of judgement Jesus will say to his people, 'Well done, good and faithful servant; you have been faithful over a few things, I will make you ruler over many things. Enter into the joy of your Lord' (Matt. 25:23). Our God is a gracious and kind

Master who treats us far beyond anything we could ever hope for. For when we served Satan we found out that he is a hard taskmaster. He demands that we work hard at sinning and then he pays us the wages of misery and death. He is a cruel tyrant who, when he has ruined our health and our lives, sees us cast into hell and cares nothing more for us.

But not so our loving Father in heaven! We love to serve him in gratitude because he purchased us from the slavery of sin through the blood of his own Son. And he has given us the privilege of serving in his house where we are joyfully and gainfully employed. Instead of death we are the heirs of eternal life. It is a free gift. It is not something we earn by serving him. Every blessing we receive in his employment is of grace. And that is why the psalmist says, 'I would rather be a doorkeeper in the house of my God than dwell in the tents of wickedness' (Ps. 84:10). It is better to burn out for Christ on earth than to burn in hell with the devil. It is better to be God's servant than Satan's sweetheart. For God is not an ogre but infinitely kind.

Now as simple as this statement in Luke 17:10 is, it has great implications for our lives.

1. We cannot accumulate merit with God by our good works

The first implication has to do with the error that we think we can accumulate merit with God by our good works. Roman Catholics believe that some people, by taking vows of poverty and celibacy and living devout lives, can do more than God requires. These extra good works can earn merit for them before God and then can be passed on to those who have not done their duty to God, provided that they pray to these so-called saints for the transfer of the additional merit to them. The Church of Rome calls them 'works of supererogation'. But Luke 17:10 says that it is impossible for a Christian to perform any works that are over and above what God requires. We are all unprofitable servants because profit does not begin until a servant goes beyond what is required of him. The word servant here is the word for a slave, and a slave owes his master everything. Leon Morris, in his commentary says, 'Our best service does not give us a claim on God.'

Moreover, even after we are converted we all continue to sin and come short of the glory of God, and it is only the infinitely meritorious work of Christ's sinless life and atoning death transferred to us that can give us acceptance with God. One poet summed it up like this:

Upon a life I did not live,
    Upon a death I did not die;
Another's life, Another's death,
    I stake my whole eternity.

Salvation is all of grace for every one of us. We can never obligate God to ourselves or to anyone else. Our only hope of pardon and acceptance is in the grace and kindheartedness of God through Jesus Christ alone.

2. There is no room for pride in Christian service
A second implication of Luke 17:10 is that there is no room for pride in Christian service. When the Jews became self-satisfied and pleased with themselves, they were cut off from God's service as a nation (Matt. 21:43). But the same disaster can befall us who are Gentile Christians, says Paul: 'Do not be haughty, but fear. For if God did not spare the natural branches, he may not spare you either' (Rom. 11:20–21). The apostle did not allow even himself to become complacent. In 1 Corinthians 9:27 he says, 'But I discipline my body and bring it into subjection, lest, when I have preached to others, I myself should become disqualified [or a castaway, KJV].'

It does not matter how successful our service for God has been, whatever we accomplish is only by his grace and enabling. It is he who gives us the resources, the skill and the strength to do his work, plus the success that follows. We are only employed to do the labour. You may have served the Master for many, many years, but every morning it is your duty to get up and do 'all those things which you are commanded' to do (Luke 17:10). Self-satisfaction or complacency are not in the vocabulary of a steward of God. 'The Christian is like the ripening corn', says Thomas Guthrie, 'the riper he grows, the more lowly he bends his head.'

EXPLANATION

3. We need to have a true sense of our unworthiness
A third implication of this illustration of Jesus is for those who feel that their service is not good enough for God. If you feel that way, Jesus is saying, it is a good feeling, especially in a society obsessed with high self-esteem. Great men never think they are great and small men never think they are small. God is the only one who is worthy of being praised. We do not deserve to be praised or blessed. We have never done our duty when measured against the demands of God's Word and the example of Calvary. No matter how much we have given in terms of money, energy, time, talents, hospitality or witnessing, God deserves more and better service. It is right and proper that we should always be aware of our smallness as creatures and our unworthiness as sinners before God.

Before the Babylonians destroyed Jerusalem the Jews prided themselves on the temple that they had built for God and the service that they rendered to him there. They felt that God should be indebted to them for all that they and their fathers had done for him. They thought that God would never allow the city to fall into the hands of pagans. But in Isaiah God says,

Heaven is my throne,
    And earth is my footstool.
Where is the house that you will build me?
    And where is the place of my rest?
For all those things my hand has made,
    And all those things exist (Isa. 66:1–2).

In other words, I gave you the strength and skill and riches to build this temple — without me you could never have done it. So, I am not in the least bit obligated to dwell there or to protect it. Where then will God be pleased to dwell? On whom will he look with favour? God says,

But on this one will I look:
On him who is poor and of a contrite spirit,
And who trembles at my word (Isa. 66:2)

EXPLANATION

A true sense of our unworthiness is the work of God's grace in our soul. It is pleasing in his sight because it points to him as the source. To quote Thomas Manton, 'The best of God's people have abhorred themselves. Like the spire of a steeple, we are least at the highest.' So do not be discouraged but rather take comfort in the fact that you are seeing things as they really are. It is right and proper for us to know that whereas God owes us nothing, we owe him everything. Such was the attitude of Robert Murray M'Cheyne who said, 'Oh for true, unfeigned humility! I know I have cause to be humble; and yet I do not know one half of that cause. I know I am proud; and yet I do not know the half of that pride.'

Let that be the spirit in which all of us, who are stewards of God under grace, will go out each day we have left on earth to do the work that our heavenly Master has commanded us to do. The Lord grant that it may be so.

KEY THOUGHTS

In the eyes of the world the best entertainers, athletes, politicians and military leaders are those who come across as brash, self-confident and boastful; humility is a sign of weakness, a lack of confidence and poor self-worth. In the eyes of God pride in yourself and your achievements is detestable because it is a wilful failure to acknowledge that your life, your gifts and your success are all due to the undeserved goodness of your almighty Creator and Redeemer. Christlike humility, however, is both a garment and an ornament that he loves to behold on his servants.

———

Arrogancy is a weed that ever grows in dunghills.
— *George Swinnock*

Pride is a sin the Lord hates, because it is a sin that sets itself most against him. Other sins are against God's laws, this is against his being and sovereignty.'
— *Spiros Zodhaites*

QUESTIONS FOR DISCUSSION

1. *Is there any place for pride or self-satisfaction in a Christian's service to God? Read Isaiah 6:1–9; 66:1–2; Romans 12:3; Philippians 3:1–16 and give as many reasons as you can find in these passages or elsewhere to substantiate your answer.*

2. *In Romans 12:3 Paul says we ought to 'think soberly, as*

God has dealt to each one a measure of faith'.
What does he mean by 'a measure of faith' and
how does it affect our attitude to ourselves?

3. Read Luke 12:35–37; 17:7–10; Matthew 25:14–23;
   Romans 11:20–22 and answer the following questions:
   a. Can we put God in our debt by faithfully serving
      him?
   b. Is God unappreciative of our service to him?
   c. Should we ever be satisfied with our service to
      God?

4. Dr Martyn Lloyd-Jones once said, 'We can be proud
   of our humility, indeed I think we always are if we try
   to give the impression of humility.' Is this a danger
   we need to guard against?

SUGGESTIONS FOR PRAYER

1. Confess to God your sin of pride and self-satisfaction
   concerning your life and service for him.

2. Ask him to give you the mind of Christ as depicted
   by Paul in Philippians 2:3–8.

To find out more about other titles
in *The Guide* series, or to ask a question,
please go to our web site

www.evangelicalpress.org/TheGuide